Winning the
Game of Belief

Winning the Game of Belief

Cultivating the Cultural Grit that Defines America's Greatest Coaches

Kevin Sheehan

With Charles Sullivan

ROWMAN & LITTLEFIELD
Lanham • Boulder • New York • London

Published by Rowman & Littlefield
An imprint of The Rowman & Littlefield Publishing Group, Inc.
4501 Forbes Boulevard, Suite 200, Lanham, Maryland 20706
www.rowman.com

6 Tinworth Street, London SE11 5AL, United Kingdom

British Library Cataloguing in Publication Information Available

Library of Congress Cataloging-in-Publication Data

978-1-4758-4899-1 (cloth)
978-1-4758-4901-0 (paper)
978-1-4758-4900-4 (electronic)

∞™ The paper used in this publication meets the minimum requirements of American National Standard for Information Sciences—Permanence of Paper for Printed Library Materials, ANSI/NISO Z39.48-1992.

To Frank Januszewski, and all of the coaches in my life, who valiantly struggled to nurture belief when times were darkest. To my wife, Irene, the major hope creator in my life, who has enabled me to win the game of belief against all odds, the inspiration for our *cultural grit*, the passion that drives and defines our three sons, Ryan, Dylan, and Casey

—K.P.S.

To Robert and Mary E. Sullivan, my mom and dad, and my great team at home, Maggie, my wife and our captain, and my three children, Fionnual, Patrick, and Caeli, who are warriors. Love you all.

—C. S.

Contents

Part III: Maintaining Belief

Foreword

Brian Magoffin

*B*elieve. It sounds easy enough. And frankly, when the top-seeded Springfield College men's basketball team was upset in overtime on their home court in Blake Arena in the New England Women's and Men's Athletic Conference (NEWMAC) Championship Semifinals on February 24, 2018, many believed that their dreams of reaching the NCAA Division III Championship Tournament had come to an end.

But two days later, after Springfield was the last team announced on the national selection show, there was an eruption of jubilation from a group of twelve student-athletes and five coaches. Many in that room knew they had the talent to make a deep postseason run. But did they truly believe?

Enter Charlie Sullivan. The Springfield College men's volleyball coach, who some considered to be one of the finest coaches in all of America, regardless of sport or division, believed he could help this group; fifteen minutes into their next practice, he did just that, and the rest is history.

The team traveled down to Philadelphia and pulled out wins over Albright and nationally ranked Cabrini to reach the Sweet Sixteen. But how did he do it, what did he say to get them to believe? The following Monday on campus, you know who was waiting for them at practice, "And to think, guys, I haven't even given you the good stuff yet. Last week was just a taste of how I can help."

Four days later, trailing by eight with 1:42 left, the belief never wavered. Down five with thirty-two seconds left, they knew they were still in it. Facing a three-point deficit with three seconds left and an opposing player at the free-throw line, believing was still on everyone's mind. And after two missed free throws, Andy McNulty believed his three-point bid from thirty-five feet at the buzzer was going to find the bottom of the net to force overtime. You better believe it did.

A win in overtime against nationally ranked Hamilton and a triumph the following night over host and fourteenth-ranked Swarthmore allowed Springfield to reach their first ever NCAA Championship Final Four in program history. Quite the accomplishment, considering the school is the *Birthplace of Basketball.*

I've seen it happen countless times and been blessed to witness Charlie Sullivan interact with his student-athletes, dissect opponents, and continue to reinvent the ways in which he gets the most out of people around him. His message and insight transcends the game of volleyball, and goes beyond athletics. His focus on creating a culture of belief and understanding how adhering to a process facilitates reaching an end product can help any of us in business, teaching, or being parents.

While his stories in the chapters to follow are entertaining and inspiring, the true essence of this book lies in all of us scratching the surface of believing in others and ourselves. After dropping the first set of the 2017 NCAA Division III National Championship in front of sold-out crowd at home in Blake Arena, Springfield College's body language and play was more than suspect.

As the second set began to play out, it appeared as though this opportunity to win a title on their home court was going to slip away from the Pride. I'll never forget that moment as I sat just feet from Sullivan at my spot on the scorers tables. We'd spent hundreds of matches together in our relationship as head coach and director of sports communications, but how the next interaction played out was out of the ordinary.

Over the years, we've shared laughs on the sidelines, and as the years progressed, I'd become more zealous in providing plenty of unsolicited advice. "Bri', I don't know if this one's gonna happen. I don't think we've got what it takes today. What do you think?" he asked as the crowd was just waiting for an opportunity to erupt and aid their classmates to a win.

One of the greatest coaching minds the sport has ever seen wondered what I thought? "Coach, you've got to believe—you've got to get these guys going. Make them remember how special they are, how dynamic this offense can be. This is on you now. Coach, you've got to make this happen. And it starts with getting number 5 to believe that he is the best player in the country."

Had I overstepped? Maybe. But at that moment, Charlie needed to get number 5, Ricky Vega, to *believe.* Just days removed from being named the Division III National Player of the Year, Ricky's flare for the dramatic, coupled with sensational leaping ability and a whip of a right arm would be the reason Springfield had a chance to change the mood in Blake Arena.

And with that, he called timeout, trailing 17–16. The team retreated to the bench, and Sullivan stood alone with Vega on the sideline. The light bulb had gone off; the power of belief was able to take a stranglehold of the match. Six points later, Vega elevated for a thunderous solo block to give Springfield a lead it would not relinquish as it escaped the second set with a win before cruising to a four-set victory over New Paltz as the Pride won their tenth national title in program history and Vega garnered his third MVP recognition of a NCAA Championship.

I just wish Charlie had been mic'd up by the NCAA broadcast so I could have heard what he said to Ricky. At his core, Sullivan is a teacher. His approach to recruiting boys volleyball players to Springfield College and helping them believe in themselves as they develop into leaders in their field, as well as future husbands and fathers, is a model to follow. Whether a CEO of a major corporation or an elementary school physical education teacher, harnessing the power of belief to elevate those around us is paramount. For the past decade, I'm proud to say I've been there by his side to support him in his run of unprecedented successes. Be it the national championship victories, being on staff of the U.S. National Team as they captured the bronze medal at the 2016 Olympics, or developing the most All-Americans in Division III volleyball history, I fully believe that Charlie Sullivan has captured something special, and there is no doubt that he will make a difference in your life, just as he has in mine.

Acknowledgments

We would like to thank both Springfield College and Molloy College for their support in providing the foundation and the forum that allowed this work to grow. Springfield College provided the stage for the amazing experiences written about in the course of this book. A special thank you must go to Dr. Mary Beth Copper, president of Springfield College, for her support of and devotion to the program. Despite ushering in an unprecedented era of growth at Springfield College, Dr. Cooper always finds the time to be there for the student athletes on the team and never misses those final games at the end of every season.

Thanks must also go to Dr. Craig Poisson, Springfield College's athletic director, for his never-ending support of the volleyball programs and all the programs that define the spirit, mind, body, and philosophy that shape every team at the college. A special thank-you is owed legendary Springfield lacrosse coach, Keith Bugbee, who had the courage to open his program to the game of belief and whose teams provide the foundation for many of the lessons that define this book. We would be remiss not to mention the extraordinary contributions of Brian Magoffin, Springfield College assistant athletic director for communications, who wrote the foreword and who has been on this journey with Coach Sullivan and the volleyball program every step of the way.

Molloy College's thirst for new knowledge and for transformative experiences provided the spark that ignited this book. A special thank-you is extended to Dr. Drew Bogner, president of Molloy College, for being the source of that spark and, most certainly, gratitude and thanks must be extended to the faculty sabbatical committee for providing the opportunity for this research to take place by providing the gift of time.

A special thank-you is owed to our tireless Molloy College graduate assistant, Gabriela Batista, for completing a host of behind-the-scenes tasks that made this book possible. Gabby was responsible for the real heavy lifting in the organization of this book, with jobs too numerous to name, not only making them look easy, but with a never-ending smile on her face.

Finally, a debt of gratitude is owed to the extraordinary athletes, coaches, and support staff who make up the Springfield volleyball program for providing the stage and the stories that bring to life the power of belief and who have forged an unbelievable culture of grit that defines Springfield College Volleyball.

Introduction

The Magic of Stories

Trying to teach an abstract principle without a concrete foundation is like trying to start a house by building the roof in the air.

—Chip and Dan Heath

I do believe in the power of story. I believe that stories have an important role to play in the formation of human beings, that they can stimulate, amaze, and inspire their listeners.

—Hayao Miyazaki

Humans live in landscapes of make-believe. We spin fantasies. We devour novels, films, and plays. Even sporting events and criminal trials unfold as narratives. Yet the world of story has long remained an undiscovered and unmapped country. It's easy to say that humans are "wired" for story. . . . Human minds yield helplessly to the suction of a story.

—Jonathan Gottschall

RESEARCH WITHOUT GOING TO THE DENTIST'S OFFICE

If you want to see a shiver of panic run thorough an audience listening to a talk on leadership and the psychology that drives it, announce to the attendees that you are about to share the details of the collected research studies that support the topic. The reaction you get will not be unlike your own response to your dentist when told that you will experience a little discomfort on the next dental procedure, a root canal.

Rather than taking you to a dentist's office in this book's exploration of leadership and the new world of positive psychology, this narrative will share actual stories and metaphors used by Charlie Sullivan and America's coaching legends to impart belief. These stories provide the vehicle to bring the research to life. The original research studies that support the theories are published and available but are generally absent from this text.

This book attempts to share the psychology of winning coaches by bringing you into locker rooms to experience what is said in those rooms and get a sense of the imagery and core values that winning coaches employ to inspire belief in their teams. Hopefully, as you read on, those stories can be permanently encoded in your brain as they were in the minds of the players who were inspired by them.

BRAIN RESEARCH: THE FRAGILE NATURE OF MEMORY

The reason for presenting research through stories emanates from the emerging neuroscience research on how the brain learns. Simply put, our brains are more engaged by hearing stories than in recalling declarative information. Stories, not research studies, stick with us far longer than statistics from a PowerPoint slide. Think back to the pressure-packed day when you entered a classroom with all of the information for the big test tenuously encoded in your brain.

On the day of that test, it would not be uncommon for you and your classmates on entering the classroom to urge the teacher in frenzied, panicked tones to administer the test immediately. After hours of study and preparation for the test, your anxious classmates might blurt out, "Please, give us the test right now, don't talk to us." Students, in this hour of anxiety and urgency, can feel the fragile nature of the isolated facts that they have stored in memory for recall on the test.

There is a recognition that these now vital facts will soon be deleted and replaced by other facts. Even the talk of the teacher on final details can dislodge key information precariously stored for the test. This demand on the teacher for a quick delivery of the impending assessment is a concrete verbalization of the perceived and accurate reality that the facts that the students have crammed into memory will soon be discarded.

Although the most flattering metaphor describes the brain as a sponge, the reality is that it is more like a sieve, discarding massive amounts of unused information to make room for new information at an alarming rate. The brain does not have the memory space to hold all the images and information that it is bombarded with, so memory for details is fragile. The brain is actively discarding information as rapidly as it is taking in new information.

Stories, however, are stored differently. Stanford University's Chip Heath and brother Dan Heath, in *Made to Stick: Why Some Ideas Survive and Others Die*, make the case that our brain's primary method of making sense of the world around us is through stories. We are more able to remember the story of Subway sandwich's power to help us lose weight through the vehicle of its classic story of Jared than by a listing of calorie counts that are connected with each of Subway's sandwich choices.

Although we might not remember the exact sandwich choice associated with Jared's successful weight loss, we seem to permanently remember his name, and, more importantly, *his weight-loss story*. What emerges from the Heath research is that stories remain in memory far longer than details and facts. It logically follows that if we want to retain information, we should present the information in a story.

The fear of this book is that after being totally motivated by the powerful lessons that demystify why some coaches win all the time, your brain will make room for new information in the same way as it did after the big test, by discarding the information from memory. For this reason, each chapter is introduced by an engaging story that encapsulates the meaning behind the theory.

We are confident that although you may not recall all the details of each section of the book, you will never forget the stories that begin each chapter. We can guarantee the Coach Sullivan stories that drive this book will be truly unforgettable. Whenever I share these stories of how Coach Sullivan inspires belief in his team, generally over a Coca Cola or adult beverage or two, I have a rapt audience.

The hope is that these stories will not only stay with you long after your reading, but will also become your teaching metaphors to inspire your teams. Although you might forget the details and the research associated with a psychological construct or chapter heading, the stories shared will *stick* with you forever.

Since a good teacher is a good thief, you are invited and encouraged to steal the stories and the metaphors behind those stories. You are encouraged to use these same stories to impart to your *teams or organizations* in order to win the game of belief.

WHAT HAPPENS TO OUR BRAIN IN A STORY?

Sarah Doody, in her *New York Times* article, "What Science Says about the Effect of Stories on our Brains," contends that when we hear a story, *we actually experience the story as if it were happening to us*. Hearing or reading a story involves stimulating the same areas of the brain that would be involved if you were in the story yourself. Through stories, our brains visualize, hear, touch, smell, and feel, not just in our imaginations, but through the activation of brain function.

If you are one of those people who struggle with the process of re-creating a story in your own imagination, through the magic of QR Codes, there are times in this book that you can authentically be a part of the action by truly being in the room with the coaches or researchers at the core of the work.

All you need do is to download the QR Reader application on your phone, and you can be magically transported to the front lines for a front-row seat. Don't worry, for those of you to whom QR codes are a foreign language, we will provide a website with links to insure that you are connected. This text will be accompanied by a website, *WinningtheGameofBelief.com*, which will maintain the links for you as time goes by.

WHO IS CHARLIE SULLIVAN?

There is a good chance that, unless you are a serious volleyball aficionado, you have never heard of Charlie Sullivan and his incredible record in coaching volleyball at Springfield College in Massachusetts. Our journey on winning the game of belief begins with Coach Sullivan after his Springfield graduation, struggling to find his way as a professional soccer player in Europe.

The *story* of a how a coin toss changed his life begins our book and is a story that should stay with you long after the book. The secret of Charlie Sullivan's successes can accessed through the stories that he has created to translate his core values into action, and this story sets the tone for your introduction to the game of belief.

What you will soon discover is that the core values that explain Coach Sullivan's unbelievable record at Springfield are the same core values that describe any organization that wins consistently. Powerful brain chemicals have encoded his stories in the brains of his players forever, and soon they will be encrypted in your memory. Before this introduction become too much like the visit to the dentist's office that I warned you about, we will begin by sharing the story of Charlie Sullivan,

Even though you know little about Charlie Sullivan at this point, I am betting that you will be engaged when you hear the story of how a lost coin toss can change a life. Let your imagination transport you to Charlie Sullivan and his game of belief. Enjoy the stories and the ride that they will take you on. What is different about this book is that it takes you behind the headlines and scores to offer you a different perspective on coaches who win all the time.

Harnessing the research and power of positive psychology, what follows will not be about specific strategies or game adjustments, but will reveal how America's greatest coaches also win the game of belief. Knowing that our minds can wander as we read and we can forget the key ideas, each chapter will end with five takeaways and a concise summary of the big idea that the chapter seeks to impart. As mentioned earlier, the brain is more of a sieve than a sponge. Now, let's meet Coach Sullivan.

Five Takeaways from *The Power of Stories*

1. Truly effective leaders, in all fields, communicate their core values through stories and metaphors.
2. According to Heath and Heath, the brain makes sense of the world around us through stories. Stories tend to stick in memory, while the facts that surround those stories may soon be discarded. We seem able to retain stories forever, while often discarding the details behind those stories.
3. When individuals hear or read a story, it is as if they are experiencing that story in their own lives. The same areas that would activate in life are stimulated in the brain as we read a story.
4. Winning coaches harness the power of positive psychology to bring out the best in each of the individuals that make up their organizations.
5. Leaders, outside of coaching, can employ the same stories and core beliefs at the heart of America's most successful sports teams to transform their business into organizations that win all the time.

The Big Idea from *The Power of Stories*

Brain research has discovered that the most effective way to communicate messages that will impart deep and lasting belief in an organization is through the power of stories. The secrets of winning the game of belief will be shared through the power of the stories that begin each chapter.

I

BEYOND WINNING

The Culture of Winning

Good enough is neither good nor enough.

—Charles Sullivan, Springfield College Volleyball, Core Values 2016–2017

Champions aren't made in gyms. Champions are made from something they have deep inside them—a desire, a dream, a vision. They have to have last-minute stamina, they have to be a little faster, they have to have the skill and the will. But the will must be stronger than the skill.

—Muhammad Ali

You were born to win, but to be a winner you must plan to win, prepare to win, and expect to win.

—Zig Ziglar

SPRINGFIELD VOLLEYBALL: A CULTURE OF WINNING

The date is April 30, 2017, and the place is Springfield College's sold-out Blake Arena, the legendary birthplace of volleyball. As the final serve of the opposing New Paltz team smashes into the net and the official awards the final point and the match to the Springfield team, the overflow crowd of students, faculty, and spectators rushes onto the volleyball court and dances with the victorious team as the music blares out the lyrics of Darius's Rucker's, "Wagon Wheel."

The gym is physically rocking like a wagon wheel with the pure euphoria of another national volleyball championship, and for Springfield College and their legendary coach, Charlie Sullivan, this is not an unusual occurrence. To go beyond reading to feel the excitement championship volleyball generates, you can join Coach Sullivan and the Springfield team at that NCAA final by accessing the video of the event through the QR Code below or by accessing the link into your browser.

Figure 1.1.   2017 NCAA National Championship Volleyball: Springfield College versus New Paltz College. Author created.

Championships in volleyball are events that seem to happen nearly every year at Springfield College. The Springfield men's volleyball coach has become a legend in the sport of volleyball. Coach Sullivan has certainly earned the title of a coach that wins all the time. Springfield College men's volleyball team, under Coach Charles Sullivan, has won more Division III National Championships than any other program in the sport's history.

The Springfield Pride have raised the championship trophy eleven times, including five out of the last seven years. The Springfield volleyball team meets the criteria for a team that wins all of the time. To validate this claim, review the record of Springfield College over the last seven years. As you read through the statistics, pay especially close attention to Coach Sullivan's own words about the origins of his success shared on the very last line of the analysis.

What should have grabbed your attention was that Coach Sullivan claims that his amazing record has nothing to do with volleyball. Why would such an iconic coach of a nationally prominent program make this incredible claim about the team's unprecedented string of championship seasons? If this run of championships has nothing to do with volleyball, then what does it have to do with?

That enigmatic statement has hopefully piqued your curiosity and imagination, and the answer to that question and the validation of Coach Sullivan's last line is what we hope to uncover in this book. Springfield College, known as the birthplace of basketball, is one of the leading physical education schools in America and has a reputation for excellence in Division III athletics in nearly every sport.

Athletic success at Springfield defines many of the college's athletic programs. For example, Keith Bugbee's renowned Springfield lacrosse team has made the NCAA playoffs for eleven straight years and has produced so many college coaches that *Inside Lacrosse* refers to the coaches from the college as

2012 – 2018 vs Div. III Opponents

Year	Record	April Record	Final Result
2012	33-1	8-0	Won National Championship
2013	32-1	9-0	Won National Championship
2014	27-3	8-1	Won National Championship
2015	25-3	8-1	National Championship Final
2016	28-3	5-2	National Championship Final
2017	29-1	6-1	Won National Championship
2018	31-0	7-0	Won National Championship
TOTAL	*205-12 (94%)*	*49-5*	**NOTHING TO DO WITH VOLLEYBALL**

Figure 1.2.   Charles Sullivan Presentation to CONVENE. Author created.

The Springfield Mafia. The school has the reputation for producing the best physical education teachers in America. However, volleyball's run of national championships is unmatched in the school's renowned history.

Springfield College is an NCAA Division III School and by collegiate rules can give no financial aid for athletic prowess or achievement. The university supports the volleyball program in ways that are similar to how it supports all of its programs. There has been no special initiative or emphasis by the administration to win in volleyball above any other sport.

Looking at winning through the lens of Springfield's extraordinary coach, this book examines why some teams seem to win nearly all the time. Rather than deal with strategy or players behind the wins, this book will focus on the culture and leadership that can be found behind dynasties in sport. The hope is that the principles that drive winning in sports can be applied to any organization in any field.

WINNING COACHES UNDER THE MICROSCOPE

Some coaches win when they have that legendary player or players, those who can elevate a team to new heights. Others win in those special seasons, when all of the pieces fall into place in a given year. This is not a book about those coaches and their magical seasons. These coaches should be lauded and celebrated for those special seasons and their extraordinary success, but that will not happen in this book.

This book explores the success of Charlie Sullivan, *correlating his success with America's iconic coaches who win all time*, to uncover the source of that success. Programs, who achieve a status where their program itself becomes synonymous with winning, will be put under the microscope to discover what makes them tick.

What follows is not a celebration or a recounting of the details of any of the coaches' successes, but an attempt to analyze *why these coaches win year after year*. What is it that all these coaches and programs share? Is winning consistently a result of superior strategy, better players, more effective teaching and coaching, or is it something else, something beyond those traditional explanations?

Employing a critical lens to reveal facts that the most ardent sports fans are likely to miss, we will dig deep into why some teams win in the face of all obstacles. Certainly, this book will not be able to cover all of the coaches whose programs have become legendary and synonymous with winning. There are constantly new and exciting coaches such as Dabo Swinney of Clemson football, forging new legacies every day.

Omissions of coaches who meet the criteria is not intentional. The reader is encouraged to substitute their own favorite coaching legends for any omitted choices and see how their choices stack up in comparison to the core values of the coaches presented in the text. We are confident that those comparisons will reveal that your choice of coaches embodies the same set of values and principles as the examples we provide.

The values and principles are what you need to take away from the stories shared on winning coaches and programs. The names, sports, and eras of the coaches are almost irrelevant. Hopefully, this analysis of why these coaches win will strip away the mystique and romanticism of sports to uncover the secrets of winning outside the world of sports. The reason that this should matter to you, sports fan or not, is that when you come down to it, the secrets of winning in sports are no different than the secrets of winning in any endeavor in life.

WHY IS IT SOME COACHES SEEM TO WIN ALL THE TIME?

The above question has been posed to capture the attention and stimulate the curiosity of anyone reading this text. Why is it that certain coaches and teams seem to win year in year out, almost regardless of who plays for the teams? Teams certainly do not win without exceptional athletes, but every year, there are teams with extraordinary talent and great players who do not win.

Springfield College is certainly blessed with fantastic players, as are all teams who win all the time. But teams and coaches who win consistently seem almost to win regardless of who plays for them. With graduation every year, the rest of the country usually feels that this might be their year as Springfield generally loses extraordinary athletes—and in most years, the national player of the year. What happens the next year is that a new set of players rises to that same level of performance.

If the winning is not solely about the best players, is the winning a result of exceptional strategy, strategy that is superior to that employed by rival coaches that makes the differences for these teams and coaches? Certainly, coaches that win all the time have truly sound and exceptional strategy, and *an ability to adapt their strategy to every situation*. But, does the difference between winning and losing reside in superior strategy alone?

If winning were merely about the right strategies, wouldn't teams simply emulate and employ those same winning strategies to negate the advantage? Or is it, as Nick Saban, the Alabama football coach contends, merely an unmatched work ethic that wins the championships? There is no doubt that teams that win consistently have a superior work ethic, but can it be that simple? Is it that teams that win all the time simply work harder than the other teams?

Bear in mind that there are many teams possessed with superior work ethic that do not win at all. Winning teams are not always the teams that have worked the hardest. Maybe, teams that win all the time have all three of the components, superior players, strategy, and work ethic. But I bet we can name teams with all three of the above characteristics—players, strategy, and work ethic—that are not at the top of the standings at the end of competition.

This book will propose that Charlie Sullivan and that teams that win all the time, *win the game of belief.* The culture of these teams and teams that win all the time instill unshakable belief in their team members and in their ultimate success. How they do that is what we hope to share in the pages that follow is the pathway to creating that culture of belief.

WINNING THE GAME OF BELIEF

In the simplest terms, teams that win all the time, have a greater belief that they will win than the teams that they play. Teams that win all the time believe, and that belief is unwavering, no matter what obstacles arise in a game, no matter what challenges they face. Analyzing the practices that grow this belief in their players will reveal how these teams become empowered through belief.

Why you need this book more than you might think at the present moment is because we all play this same game of belief every day. Even though you may not be aware of the game, you are playing it, and the outcome of our game of belief dictates the quality of your life, work, and relationships.

The belief game is not centered on religious beliefs or the great mysteries of life, but focuses on what we believe our future to be. The stronger and more unwavering our belief in our future success is, the more likely it is that we achieve our goals. Lose belief and everything is lost. This is a book that shares the secrets of how to win that game of belief that you wage in your life on a daily basis and how to impart the secrets of winning that game to all in your organizations.

The narrative centers around one extraordinary coach and cross-references his success with the practices and experiences of legendary coaches in other sports who win all the time. This cross-referencing is designed to reveal the formula for winning the game of belief that is shared by all of these coaches. Think of the stories about Charlie Sullivan and of the iconic coaches that follow as a how-to manual for life that has been derived from an analysis of their core values.

The shared core of values of these extraordinarily different coaches can create a winning culture in your organization. The case of Charles Sullivan's success in volleyball seems to defy all conventional wisdom about success in sport, but you will discover the story of his success is not at all unprecedented in coaching icons. In fact, the success of Springfield volleyball is more the norm than the exception. We hope the stories inspire you to begin your own story. Sit back and enjoy your front-row seat on the success of Coach Sullivan. Welcome to the game of belief.

Five Takeaways from *The Culture of Winning*

1. Coaches and leaders, who win all the time, win the game of belief by creating in their members an unshakeble belief that they can overcome any obstacle that they face.
2. Coaches who win all the time win not just because of greater players, superior strategy, or an unparalleled work ethic. They win because they have superior belief in their ultimate success.
3. Although coaches who win all the time vary in sport, strategy, practices, and temperament, if you strip away the surface differences, you will discover remarkable shared similarities in the core values of each team.
4. Maintaining belief in the face of setbacks is the key to winning the game of belief. Coaches who win all the time employ a set of practices that arm their players to face challenges without wavering.
5. Coaches who win all the time are more successful because of their ability to instill in their teams a set of principles that inspire belief.

The Big Idea from *The Culture of Winning*

Organizations that win all the time foster in their members an unshakable belief that they will triumph in the end. *They win the game of belief.* This belief is tested on a daily basis and the role of any leader is to arm his members with the belief that they can overcome any obstacle or challenge that they face in their pursuit of excellence.

Welcome to the Game of Belief

Lacrosse is over, welcome to the game of belief.

—Phone Taping of Charles Sullivan's Address
to Springfield College Lacrosse Team 2015

Success is an attitude, a mindset, a decision, a commitment, a promise. A belief that it can be done, should be done, and WILL be done.

—George Akomas Jr.

First comes thought; then organization of that thought, into ideas and plans; then transformation of those plans into reality. The beginning, as you will observe, is in your imagination.

—Napoleon Hill

MEET CHARLIE SULLIVAN:
WELCOME TO THE GAME OF BELIEF

Cell phones are pretty amazing devices. Not only can they take pictures, play music, and map out directions, but they can also record conversations, speeches, and lectures. As my son, Dylan Sheehan, waited in the locker room on the eve of his 2015 NCAA lacrosse playoff game with local rival Western New England University, he knew the pregame talk of Coach Sullivan might be one that had a tremendous impact on the game, and maybe, on his life. He could not have known that his recording of that talk would be the impetus for this book.

Western New England University had easily handled Springfield College in their regular season game, and the mood of the team on the eve of the game was somewhat apprehensive and tense. The team awaited the arrival of Coach Sullivan with some trepidation. Coach Sullivan's talks had become a tradition for NCAA bound teams at Springfield College. But if you somehow could have had a window into the subconscious and revealed the team's hidden beliefs, the room would have housed a good deal of doubt.

As a student in Coach Sullivan's sport psychology class, and knowing that Coach Sullivan's theories were parallel to my current doctoral research on hope and grit, my son decided to tape that talk on his phone. There was no way at that time that either of us could have predicted the effects that would extend far beyond lacrosse fields and volleyball courts. Let me take you back to the talk, and let's listen in on Coach Sullivan's address to the lacrosse team.

"What am I doing here?" the charismatic Springfield volleyball coach asked the college's assembled lacrosse team, as they sat huddled on the eve of this first-round NCAA playoff game. The players' responses were mumbled and muffled, but mostly inaudible. The team was all too familiar with the speaker as the college's legendary volleyball coach, and Coach Sullivan was respected as one of their school's most popular and renowned sports psychology professors, but their responses to the coach's questions were unsure and inaudible.

The coach continued, now a bit more loudly and aggressively, posing the same question again. "Seriously fellows, I am paying a babysitter fifteen dollars an hour and she won't even do a dish. I am going home to a sink full of dirty dishes, so what I am doing here?" The players now mumbled in voices that began to take a form that could now be deciphered, "Big game tomorrow, Coach."

The volleyball coach now sarcastically chastised the team. "I know you have a big game, I have seen you on social media, followed your tweets, and I know that you have a big game, *but what I am doing here?*" Somewhat sheepishly, the team responded, "We want to win, Coach."

Coach Sullivan continued, "Sure you want to win, *and they want to win.* You've had a good season, *and they have had a good season, too.* I know, I know, you're a family, *but they are a family as well.* I got news for you, boys, the game of lacrosse is over. Sorry to tell you, especially you seniors, but the game of lacrosse ended with your last week. The goals you scored, the games you won, they are now in the past. *Lacrosse is officially over; welcome to the game of belief.*"

Stunned by such an out-of-the box pronouncement, the team sat transfixed, eager to learn, if lacrosse was over, what was tomorrow all about? Sullivan went on, "What we have tomorrow fellows is the game of belief, and it's a simple game. If you believe more than they do, you'll win."

This was my introduction to Coach Sullivan, and it came through that muffled telephone recording that my son made for me on the eve of one of their biggest playoff games in his sophomore year at the college. This was not an unusual event, as Coach Sullivan speaks to most of the teams at Springfield College that are scheduled to make an NCAA tournament appearance.

There is good reason for pregame inspirational talks by Coach Sullivan, as the teams that he addresses are 24–1 after these pregame talks. The one defeat was not a surprise to the coach, as he warned the coach of that team. *"Your best player is not buying in. She does not believe. Your team cannot win the game of belief, when your leader does not buy in."*

In this brief talk to the lacrosse team, Coach Sullivan deftly wove the fabric of belief into the lacrosse team's culture. The talk promised that belief that would guarantee a successful outcome the next day. All the players had to do was to hold fast to their belief in the face of the obstacles that would test that belief.

Losing a faceoff or falling behind by a goal were defined as obstacles, threats to belief. He armed the team with ways to support each other in the face of any setback in the game that might lessen their belief. The belief that a team carries into a game is an expected commodity that is hoped for, but rarely talked about by coaches *as the essential ingredient necessary for victory.*

Coach Sullivan made maintaining the team's belief in their success into the most important thing in this game on this day. Coach Sullivan then went on to mathematically spell out the power of belief through an equation in which he predicted the score of the game based only on the difference in belief levels of each team.

There is a way for you to dominate, play your best, play fast, lightning quick. Want to dominate, want to win? Here's the deal. . . . There is a way to do that, and fortunately not everyone in the NCAA tournament knows how to do that. It's not that hard. The only thing that matters is the game of belief. In the game of belief . . . if you believe more than they do, you will win. If you believe at 55 percent and they at 45 percent, you will win 10 to 9. If you believe at 60 percent and they at 40 percent, you will win 12 to 8. If you believe at 70 percent and they at 30 percent, you will win 14 to 7. If you believe at 90 percent and your opponent believes at 10 percent, you will win 15 to 3. Guaranteed.

If you want to experience this amazing talk rather than read about it, through the magic of YouTube and QR codes, you can actually hear the same talk that the team experienced in this pregame address on the power of belief. Although the recording is a bit muffled, what comes through is the inspirational power of belief and the magic of Coach Sullivan in inspiring that belief.

Figure 2.1.   Pregame Recording of Coach Sullivan's talk to the Springfield Lacrosse Team on the Eve of NCAA Playoff Game (2015) (https://youtu.be/_3RlMUlLhx8). Author created.

That cell phone recording was my introduction to Coach Sullivan and the culture of belief that he creates at Springfield College. It became exceedingly obvious that his brief talk was about creating not just individual belief but a cultural belief that could only be effective if shared by all members of the team. It was also immediately obvious to me that this culture, built on belief, was about far more than sports.

Most of the serious research on speeches before major games concludes that the actual effects of such talks on outcomes, although romanticized in legend, are dramatically overrated in their actual measured effect on performance. That being said, my son's Springfield team went on to dramatically avenge their regular-season loss to Western New England the next day and cruise to an easy victory—leading by a deluge of goals at the end of the first half. They had won the game of belief on this day.

Despite what I knew about the researched effects of actual versus perceived impacts of a talk before a game, this idea of a culture of belief captured my imagination. I did next what any good coach would do. I stole the speech and this concept of a culture built on shared belief and applied the same talk to the high school lacrosse team that I was coaching.

Using Sullivan's words and the actual recording above as motivation, Massapequa High School had a very talented high school lacrosse team, but probably would not have been described as the most talented team in the state. Employing this idea that lacrosse was now a game of belief, the team went on to win the New York State championship, leading in the semifinals and finals by scores so large that the referees went to running time.

Today, those players, if asked about that magical season, would relate how the ending of that season was fueled by the strength of the *belief* that the team possessed in that playoff run and beyond. As a group, the team went on to success in high school, but their individual success on that level did not match their success as a team in high school. Could it be as simple as belief?

What struck me about this talk and its impact on results was not just the idea of individual belief, but how shared belief could transform team culture. I had to know more, so I not only listened in as Coach Sullivan addressed his team before their final game in Volleyball before the Division III National Championship in 2017, but I also had it recorded because I was not sure that I could convey the actual power of belief in words.

THE POWER OF CULTURE: YOU WERE MADE FOR THIS!

In the locker room minutes before taking to the court for the 2017 NCAA finals, the team silently sat around the coach with an air of mixed nervousness and anticipation. Coach Sullivan began, "Our culture is made for this. Our culture is built differently, and you are part of our culture. Culture defines behavior and determines how we act."

"That's what Brandon [a player from a previous team] was telling you today; that's how he won three national championships here." Coach Sullivan powerfully and deeply repeated over and over again, "Our culture is made for this. If you look at the how on the axis of our culture, you see that our culture is very fast. Kyle, you had a high ball last night. Shame on you, Kyle, you hit that ball as fast as Zooby." The team nervously smiled and laughed.

"It's efficient. Great communication. What's the language we all speak here?"

The team murmured, "Body language."

"We all speak that, and when you were getting punched in our maroon and white scrimmage, your body language was, that's a great punch. I'm going to get one, too. Stick to the game plan. Focus. Focus on what we're doing. Help each other out, but most of all, the behavior and the action of all our culture is this last one. I'm hoping you remember this from the bulletin board."

At this point, Coach Sullivan wrote on the white board, the word, *belief.* "This is all self-control. Just like we've chosen to get our bodies behind the ball, when we're serving, just like we choose to manage a bad toss, we choose, what we believe. That's how a team that's down 3 to 11 in game five wins a national championship semifinal in Blake Arena."

"You know what they said after that game?" Coach Sullivan voice lowers to a whisper that can barely be heard. "That's unbelievable. We understand you don't believe it, that's why you don't do it. That's why our culture is different. They say, *wow,* because they never tasted that before. *You were made for this.*"

"Our culture is shaped for this. You have got to believe 100 percent, no matter what happens, we got this, we can do it, we can overcome any obstacle. We can come together stronger. We can communicate better. We can move our feet more efficiently. We can be more fundamentally sound. We can figure anything out, we were made for this."

As powerful as these words are to read, there is no way that you can really experience the power of belief that the talk instilled in that team by Coach Sullivan without being in the room with his team. Through the magic of the QR code or link below, you can join the team in the locker room and feel the power of culture and of belief firsthand.

Figure 2.2. Coach Sullivan's Culture of Belief Speech Before the 2017 NCAA Volleyball Final (https://www.youtube.com/results?search_query =coach+pregame+speech+Saturday). Author created.

The chapters that follow reveal the secrets of how you can instill this culture of belief in your team, organization, or business. Although the building blocks for your culture of belief can be created through stories that originate in sport, the lessons from these stories pertain to every area of life and are validated by extensive research.

You only need the courage to begin to imagine what a culture of belief will look like in your organization or your life. Although passion and enthusiasm are present at the origin of every game, season, or project, how a team navigates and overcomes those setbacks and threats to maintain belief ultimately determines success or failure.

MORE THAN PEP TALKS: BEYOND WINNING

As inspiring and motivational as the NCAA pregame talks to other Springfield College teams were, and as impressive as the record of next-day victories were after the talks, you should be aware that these talks generally do not automatically result in NCAA championships for any of the teams other than the volleyball team.

The reason behind that disappointing statistic is that although belief can be stimulated and can begin with a talk, to be maintained in the face of threats to belief, you need a *culture* that supports belief in the face of those threats. *Belief* is a characteristic of a culture born of a set of core values that define the culture. If it were a result that could arise solely from a pregame talk or an address to a group, the book would now be completed and Coach Sullivan would be the most sought-after presenter in America.

Unshakable belief is not created in one pep talk; it needs to be a part of the fabric of every action of the team from opening meeting to final game. In this same way, in business, beliefs are an outgrowth of the culture of the business. What will become apparent is that winning in sports or succeeding in any organization is not the ultimate goal sought by truly successful coaches and leaders. Ironically, what will be revealed is that *winning* is not the goal of truly winning coaches, but only a by-product of their team principles and core values.

Truly great coaches know that the surest way *not to win* is to focus only on the goal of winning. As much as that seems counterintuitive, you will learn that single-minded focus only on the outcome or the product can be disas-trous. That focus often detracts individuals from focus on the processes that need to be mastered to obtain the end product.

Teams must adopt goals that extend far beyond winning. What *beyond winning* suggests is that the goal of developing the best *in individuals* will not only bring the success or winning we all seek, but will also provide even greater rewards. Winning is not an end goal for the most successful coaches and lead-ers, but a by-product of the process of seeking perfection in every individual.

Individuals who sacrifice personal ambitions in pursuit of that perfect process are actualized as human beings. *Beyond winning* is best expressed by analyzing the feeling that truly insightful players experience after winning a championship. There is a warm and rewarding afterglow, but almost always a feeling best expressed by the statement, "Is this all there is?"

Winning, at that moment, is suddenly revealed to not be the ultimate goal. The ultimate goal was the perfection of the process and the actualization that each player achieved in pursuit of winning, not the winning itself. Players often feel let down after finally securing a championship. There is a sudden realization that the journey to the championship that brought out the best in them and transformed them as people was far more important than a final score of the final game.

There is something more vital, beyond winning, and that something is discovering greatness in yourself. To truly create belief that lasts beyond a game or two, you have to move your team beyond winning. Coach Nick Saban, after winning his fifth national football championship in nine years at Alabama and sixth overall, clearly made the point that there is a greater goal than winning.

What made his statements and the game in question such an example of belief was that his Alabama team trailed Clemson 10 to 0 at halftime and 20 to 10 at the end of the third quarter. Saban maintains that, although sports writers like to talk about winning, there is more than just winning. His most fervent hope was that every player on his team and everyone watching the game took a lesson from his most recent championship on the resilience of the team.

In coming back from the halftime deficit, what Saban hopes sticks with players is the idea of maintaining belief in each other, never quitting, and having the persistence needed to sustain focus in the face of truly daunting setbacks. His hope was that this experience has the power to alter the life of each and every player on the team. This book shares that same hope that those lessons, forged in challenge and built on success in sports, can alter the course of your life.

Although at first glance every coach that will be referenced in this book will appear different in approach and method, on closer examination, you will discover what was discovered in researching winning cultures. Winning consistently in every situation arises from cultures that, although different, at their core are strikingly similar. In some cases, the coaches' cultures evolved independently; in other cases, the cultures were modeled after each other.

What is relevant is that these strikingly different coaches, in radically different sports, all ended up in the same place as Charlie Sullivan. Understanding the shared values and principles of these perennially winning coaches will provide a springboard for you to define and create your own core of values.

The hope is that defining your core values will move you and your organization *beyond winning*. The shared core values of these extraordinarily different coaches offer pathways for you to create a culture that moves your organization *beyond winning*. To move beyond winning is to develop in your culture the ability to overcome obstacles and setbacks.

This ability to turn obstacles into opportunities is mandatory. Every goal pursuit will be challenged by roadblocks to that goal. A leader's ability to grow from setbacks is the key winning the game of belief.

Five Takeaways from *Winning the Game of Belief*

1. Belief can be stimulated and enhanced by an increased focus, generated by a talk, but to be maintained, belief is an outcome of the core values of the culture.
2. Teams that win all the time believe that no matter what events unfold, they will win in the end. They win the game of belief. This same game of belief is played out in businesses and in every arena of our lives.
3. The surest way not to win is to focus only on winning. The most effective way to make profits is not to focus on the profit, but to focus on making the best product. In seeking to perfect the processes that lead to success, individuals are transformed as individuals. This actualization in pursuit of the perfect process changes their lives.
4. Though belief is present at the start of a game, season, or project, there will be setbacks and threats to that belief that must be overcome to maintain belief. A leader's ability in transforming obstacles into opportunities for growth is the key to winning the game of belief.
5. Leaders who inspire belief in their teams transform not only the culture of their organization, but also the lives of each member of their organization.

The Big Idea from *Winning the Game of Belief*

Teams that win all the time possess a stronger belief that they will win than the teams that they face. In the end, it is this belief that leads to success.

3

Turning Obstacles into Opportunities

The impediment to action advances action. What stands in the way becomes the way.

—Marcus Aurelius

We have to be willing to fail, to be wrong, to start again.

—Angela Lee Duckworth

When obstacles arise you change your direction to reach your goal, you do not change your decision to get there.

—Zig Ziglar

WHAT STANDS IN THE WAY BECOMES THE WAY

The impediment to action advances action. What stands in the way becomes the way. With these two sentences uttered by Marcus Aurelius, Ryan Holiday has dramatically captured the imagination of this generation in his groundbreaking work, *The Obstacle Is the Way: The Ancient Art of Turning Adversity into Advantage.* The philosophy and wisdom of Stoicism have been given new life in this inspiring treatise, urging us to view the obstacles we face as opportunities.

This profound quote empowers all of us with the secret of maintaining belief in the face of obstacles. Holiday endorses "the art of turning obstacles upside down" and suggests that seeing our roadblocks as opportunities for growth is the key to transforming "adversity into advantage."

Encountering unexpected obstacles and roadblocks might be the most apt description of Charles Sullivan's life after college and his introduction to the sport of volleyball.

In his own words, Coach Sullivan details how everything that could have gone wrong after graduation from Springfield College, *did go wrong*. Stoicism promotes the idea that these seeming obstacles, rather than "impeding your direction, are actually teaching you how to get where you want to go, carving you a path." As Coach Sullivan and America's legendary coaches reveal the stories of their beginnings, what emerges is the ability that these men share in turning obstacles into opportunities.

Charles Sullivan, recipient of USA Volleyball's All-Time Great Coach Award as a result of his being selected Division III National Coach of the Year four times, two more than any other coach and the only coach to win back-to-back years, saw his first volleyball game when he coached it. Let me repeat that so it sinks in. *The first game that Coach Sullivan ever observed was the one he coached.*

This unlikely introduction to coaching is shared not to glorify Sullivan but to convince you that your leadership is not dependent on past success in a field or natural talent. Instead, it may result more from your ability to create belief in your *team.*

As Coach Sullivan shares the stories of his entry into volleyball, you should begin to view your own challenges in this same light. Holiday suggests that we do not view obstacles as calamities but as "the opportunity to solve vexing problems with a cocktail of creativity, focus and daring. The impediment to action becomes the way."

EIGHTEEN PENCILS AND A LOST COIN TOSS: COACH SULLIVAN'S OWN WORDS ON HIS INTRODUCTION TO VOLLEYBALL

After graduation from Springfield College in 1993, I traveled to London, England, in hopes of playing soccer on a professional level. Not enjoying much success in soccer, I quickly ran out of money and crawled to the front door of an international school and asked them if I could do some work, any kind of work or manual labor for money.

At that point in my life, my goal was to be a full-time soccer player, and I was not seeking a full-time job outside of soccer, but eating did come first. The head of the school responded to my request with an offer. "We don't have any work here, but we do have a position for a physical education teacher, coach, and athletic director in our sister school in Rome, the Marymount International School for Girls."

Without hesitation, I responded, "No thank you, that is way too serious for me." But the school was desperate and my résumé was a perfect match for the job, so they flew me to Rome, Italy, for an interview. When they offered me the job, every instinct I had told me to turn them down, but there was that thing I mentioned that I have about eating.

Shortly after my taking the job, the Marymount International School for Girls decided to open its enrollment to boys to increase revenue. This addition necessitated the school now sponsoring boys' sports as well girls. I took this as a sign that my luck had turned, especially when I learned that one of the new sports to be added was *soccer*. The other sport to be added was *volleyball*.

The idea of coaching soccer seemed to me to be the opening of a new door in the face of my rapidly vanishing dreams of being a professional soccer player. The only catch to the soccer job was that, as I soon discovered, there were two males teaching at the school, and both of us were vying for this one soccer job.

In a meeting with the headmistress, I insisted that there was no way that I was coaching a boy's volleyball team. I had never even seen a volleyball match. I needed to coach soccer. Since my competitor for the position said the same thing, we decided the only fair way to decide was to flip a coin to see who would coach the soccer team and who would coach the volleyball team.

As in a Disney movie, my entire life dramatically seemed to have come down to the flip of a coin. The coin was tossed and the result did change the direction my life, but not in the expected direction. I lost that coin toss and the dreamed-of soccer position. The obstacle became the way.

This was my introduction to the world of coaching volleyball, a lost coin toss. This was a bump in the road that I never expected or saw coming. To be honest, I did not even know the rules of volleyball. When I was confused, such as when or *if* I could call a timeout, I was forced to ask our manager. To hide my lack of knowledge from the team, whenever the manager answered my rudimentary, sometimes ignorant questions, I would loudly proclaim, "Hey, that's the same as it is in America."

As our first game approached, I wanted to give our team a message that would help them play to their full potential, but the only thing I could offer them was information about team cohesion, relationships, and working hard. Being thrust into a sport that I had no knowledge of forced me to rely on creativity that I never knew I possessed.

Borrowing a lesson on the power of teamwork, I adapted a strategy from a documentary in which Isaiah Thomas's mother got the message of staying together as a family in the streets of Detroit across to her family. As I nervously addressed the team before their first game, I gave each player a pencil and asked them to break it. This they easily did, and looked at me in a bewildered way. This was not volleyball.

After each of them had broken their pencil, I called up the biggest player on the team and handed him eighteen pencils tied together in a bundle. When asked to break the eighteen pencils, the player struggled with all his might, but could not do it. I told my team that this was a demonstration that if our team played together, we would be stronger than any individual player on our team, and stronger than any player that we were going to face from the other team.

"The power of our team will diminish if our team members do their own thing. We will break like a single pencil. If we play as a team, no one can break us." My career as a volleyball coach had begun with a lost coin toss and eighteen pencils. What dawned on me after that first talk to my team was that I could learn the intricacies of volleyball, but maybe more important than volleyball strategy or knowledge were the beliefs a team held about what it takes to be successful.

After that lost coin toss and that talk, I had discovered my true passion was for coaching, and not soccer. The obstacle of not getting that soccer job provided the opportunity for strengths to emerge that might never have come to the forefront without it. Losing that coin toss turned out be the best break that I have ever received.

Not getting the soccer job provided the opportunity to look at an entirely new sport with fresh, uncharted perspectives. In fact, as a strategist for volleyball today, I believe that the fact that I did not play allows my creativity to emerge, as I am not bound by what I had learned as a player. The obstacle of not playing turned out, in some ways, to be an advantage.

LESSONS LEARNED FROM A LOST COIN TOSS: COACH SULLIVAN IN HIS OWN WORDS

This lost coin toss shattered my innate beliefs about success in coaching and opened a new door to understanding what it takes to be successful in life. The lessons learned from this lost coin toss, the loss of a desired coaching position, and the team's response to the story of the eighteen pencils taught me a good deal about turning adversity into advantage. In your life, you need to realize that the great obstacles you face are merely opportunities for inspiring your creativity and redirecting your life.

What follows in the story of our success at Springfield is not really about volleyball or any of the other sports that are referenced later. Volleyball and the world of sports are merely the laboratory for the culture and values of an organization. What you would have to conclude from my story is that I was the least likely candidate for such success in this sport. What is your story? Can you turn your obstacles into opportunity?

LESS THAN SUCCESSFUL PLAYING CAREER: OBSTACLE OR GIFT?

Isn't it a part of our American sports mythology that our greatest athletes will translate the lessons and insights gained from a lifetime of experiences in the trenches of their sport to the next generation as players? Shouldn't it make sense that the ultimate reward for a successful playing career is the platform to then share that experience, wisdom, and insight as a coach in that sport?

How could this coach, who had never played the game or even seen a game, rise to such a level of success? Sometimes losing coin tosses can provide a ticket to greatness that you never saw coming, as was the case for Charles Sullivan. Is Coach Sullivan's extreme example as a coach lacking ability, experience, and proficiency in a sport more the exception or the rule when it comes to coaches who go on to become coaching legends?

The stories of America's greatest coaches reveal that success in coaching might be negatively correlated with optimum careers as players. The lack of success as players may provide the source of burning motivation that makes coaches more creative, driven, and *passionate* about coaching. Nearly all of the perennially successful coaches that will be provided as background support in this book were not extraordinary players in their own right.

Bill Belichick was generally regarded as a far better lacrosse player than football player at Wesleyan College. In one description, it was suggested that Belichick was an ordinary Division III football player, at a less-than-recognized football school, but a far more talented lacrosse player.

Even when as a senior, when he was beaten out by a freshman for the starting defensive end spot on the Wesleyan football team, Belichick demonstrated a team-first approach. The obstacle of not starting as a senior may be the source of his team-first virtue, which today still defines Belichick's approach to coaching the New England Patriots.

Belichick's former defensive line coach and athletic director, John Biddiscombe, describes Belichick's handling of the setback of not starting in this way: "My sense is that this [his success] is all about the same type of person that he was when he wasn't a starter his senior year. He was glad to be on the team. He was a very loyal member of the team and not a complainer because he wasn't playing, and that's unusual for seniors, even in those days."

Pete Carroll, another legendary football coach, was so small in high school that he needed a doctor's note just to try out for the team in ninth grade. After two years of junior college, Pete played two years for the University of the Pacific, but injuries and a lack of speed doomed his World Football League tryout. Carroll realized that his passion for coaching the sport far outweighed his ability and natural talent as a player. His entry into coaching was fueled by his failure to earn a spot in the World Football League.

Geno Auriemma, perhaps the winningest coach in the history of women's basketball, after attending Montgomery County Community College, made the basketball team at Division III West Chester University. However, after being offered the opportunity to coach the junior varsity girls' basketball team at Bishop McDevitt High School, Geno chose to forgo his playing career and take that coaching job.

Anson Torrance, certainly America's premier women's soccer coach, was described by his father as "the most enthusiastic *untalented player* he had ever seen." At twenty-four, when a third-year law student at North Carolina, Anson was asked to coach both the men's and women's teams and found his true passion, *coaching.* Anson Torrance has won more women's soccer championships than anyone in history, but he has never argued a legal case.

With the exception of John Wooden, a three-time consensus All American at Purdue, most of the coaches referenced in this book were not legendary players in their sport. What is clear from this brief overview is that prowess in one's sport does not serve as the foundation for a Hall-of-Fame coaching career. In fact, a lack of success in one's sport instead of being an impediment to success might actually be the fuel that drives success. It can open the pathway to virtues that might otherwise never emerge. The lesson of Charles Sullivan and the lost coin toss coach is one of turning struggles into opportunities.

How do you handle failure and adversity that arise in your life? This Stoic philosophy of seeing obstacles as opportunities is now driving some of America's most successful teams, including the New England Patriots, Seattle Seahawks, Chicago Cubs, and the University of Texas men's basketball team, all of whom have read *The Obstacle Is the Way.* This same philosophy can be applied to transform the obstacles in your path to new directions.

Five Takeaways from *Turning Obstacles into Opportunities*

1. Stoicism is driven by the belief that every obstacle presents an opportunity to improve our condition. The obstacles we face are opportunities to explore new directions and pathways to success that may never have arisen without the obstacle.

2. The great majority of America's most iconic winning coaches were not gifted athletes in their sport, but emerged after less-than-successful experiences as players. The lack of innate talent in their sport may have been fuel for their passion as coaches.

3. Obstacles give rise to our virtues and creativity in adapting to adversity; we grow as individuals. According to Ben Franklin, "Things which hurt, instruct."

4. Success in leading an organization is more dependent on your ability to lead and create belief in your ability to lead than it is in your own prowess in your chosen field.

5. The most devastating setbacks we face may merely be the opening of new doorways that may never have opened if not for the hardship.

The Big Idea from *Turning Obstacles into Opportunities*

Truly successful leaders find opportunity in the obstacles that they face. In fact, the key to maintaining belief is the ability to view a setback as an opportunity for growth and to embrace the virtues that emerge as a result of the setback.

4

The Power of Personality

Effort Counts Twice

!

As much as talent counts, effort counts twice.

—Angela Lee Duckworth

It's not the will to win that matters—everyone has that. It's the will to prepare to win that matters.

—Bear Bryant

Nine years before he won the MVP (In the NBA), *as a high school senior, [Steph] Curry stood 6-feet tall and weighed 160 pounds. Famously, no power conference school offered a scholarship, not even Virginia Tech, even though his father Dell may be the best player ever to play there. Hokies* (Davidson University) *Coach Seth Greenberg offered Curry the opportunity to walk-on.*

—Adam Kilgore

The brilliance of what the Cubs did was to put their faith not just in numbers, but also in the type of people that they acquire.

—Tom Verducci, *The Cubs Way*

We've tried to find guys that have a sense about them that they can overcome whatever the odds are, and that they're going to hang through anything. And that is demonstrated in the passion that they bring to their pursuits too. It's exactly what we are looking for. We don't care what their number is in the draft class. We just want to find guys that love playing, and they've got something, and they're not going to be denied. That's really where we've tried to build a whole crew around that.

—Pete Carroll

NFL DRAFT DAY: YOU ARE ON THE CLOCK

For those of you who are not football fans, the success of a football team in the National Football League depends heavily on the team's skill and ability to draft that special quarterback. That special quarterback is the key player that the franchise believes can lead the team to a championship.

Highly paid scouts continually search out and evaluate emerging talent in the collegiate ranks, as the ultimate fate of a team resides predominantly on a franchise's ability to select that truly special quarterback. Since so much of the success of a franchise hinges on the right selection, this has become both a science and an obsession for NFL football teams.

The search for a quarterback measures a good number of variables, but prime among the attributes is physical ability. Despite extensive observation of the quarterbacks in the college ranks during the season, one of the principal evaluations is a gathering of the top candidates for an assessment of physical talent, called the combine. Combines run prospective players through a series of physical challenges and tests to measure overall athletic prowess, skill, and acumen.

Though many factors are measured aside from physical ability, including arm strength as a passer, overall collegiate success, football intelligence, and acumen, athleticism seems to be the deal breaker. A candidate's overall athleticism is the prerequisite for consideration in moving forward in a team's selection process. There is also mention and measure of coachablity and attitude, but these attributes have historically taken a secondary role to athletic prowess for nearly all teams.

Below is a chart with some of the combine scores of some the NFL's most renowned present and past NFL quarterbacks. To simulate and better understand the nature of the selection process, let's do an experiment. Pretend you are on the clock and it is selection time for you as an NFL team's general manager. Although it is difficult to pick one player based on these scores, for fun, pick the one you would choose were you made an NFL team's general manager for the day.

Write down the candidate number of your choice and save it until the end of the book to discover the actual quarterback you selected. Although players are generally not selected on the combine scores alone, they are routinely eliminated on these scores. Looking at the scores below, although it might be difficult to choose that one great quarterback on scores alone, it should be relatively easy for you as a general manager to eliminate the quarterback that most lacks the minimum athleticism to compete. After all, we have provided quantifiable measurements to support your choice.

We are putting you back on the clock again; this time, analyze the data and eliminate the quarterback that you would reject for your organization.

Without looking at the pages ahead, select that one quarterback from the seven candidates below that you would eliminate from consideration based on your evaluation of their athletic performance. After your selection, we will compare the candidate you eliminated with NFL's actual decision.

Table 4.1. NFL Draft Combine Scores

Name	40-Yard Dash	20-Yard Shuffle	3-Cone Drill	Vertical Leap
Candidate 1	4.56	4.18	6.92	35
Candidate 2	4.53	4.09	6.97	34
Candidate 3	4.53	4.18	6.85	32.5
Candidate 4	4.89	4.51	7.1	24.5
Candidate 5	5.01	4.2	7.11	30
Candidate 6	5.28	4.38	7.2	24.5
Candidate 7	4.59	4.28	6.8	36

SELECTION RESULTS: DID YOU MAKE
THE SAME DECISION AS THE NFL?

If the candidate that you chose to eliminate was Candidate 6, based on the NFL decision, you did a good job. Candidate 6 had the lowest score on nearly every measure. The NFL agreed with your selection and chose six quarterbacks in the draft before the quarterback you chose to be eliminated.

In fact, this quarterback was not chosen until *the sixth round*. It has been written that the main reason that the team chose him was because they could not believe that they could still get a potential *backup quarterback* this late in the draft. The quarterback eliminated did have some truly noteworthy and stellar performances in college, but his athletic ability was far below that of the other candidates.

His college performances had led his team to dramatic and impressive victories in his junior and senior years, but in his senior year, his college coaches decided that he would split the first half of the season with a more highly recruited freshman quarterback, who was considered a far better athlete. In essence, although this candidate had superior statistics and record for a good deal of his collegiate career, he was not considered good enough to be the starter at his own college as a senior.

The quarterbacks drafted before Candidate 6 included Chad Pennington (no. 18, First Round, Marshall University), Giovanni Carmazzi (no. 65, Third Round, Hofstra University), Chris Redmond (no. 75, Third Round, Louisville University), Tee Martin (no. 163, Fifth Round, Tennessee University), Marc

Bulger (no. 18, Sixth Round, West Virginia, University), and Spergon Wynn (no. 183, Sixth Round, University of North Texas State). This list is now legendary, but it has deeper implications.

By now, you have probably figured out that the quarterback you eliminated was Tom Brady. He was chosen in the sixth round, as the 199th player selected in the draft. How did the NFL get it so wrong? How did you eliminate such a prolific player? Not only does the NFL get it wrong, but in nearly every professional sports organization there are errors in initial selection that are equally as hard to explain.

After five Super Bowl championships, it is argued by many that Brady may be the greatest quarterback of all time. In fact, in a clear comparison with the NFL's all-time greats, Sean Glennon in *The Case for Football Greatest Quarterback: Tom Brady vs. The NFL* offers powerful statistical evidence that Brady is the greatest of all time. Why did so many teams in the National Football League pass on Tom Brady?

Sir Ken Robinson, an educational reformer from England, analyzing America's emphasis on one-size-fits-all assessments and the data in its pursuit of excellence, suggests we might be *mining the wrong data*. Robinson believes that creativity, not pure academic aptitude or achievement, are what our tests should measure. We use IQ and test scores on standardized assessments as our measuring stick for later potential in life because these are the things that are easily measured, not because they are strongly correlated with success in life.

The draft placement of Tom Brady suggests that in looking for individuals who will lead teams to greatness, the NFL may be also *be mining the wrong data*. The NFL measures time in the forty-yard dash or vertical leap, because these are the easiest things to measure. We value athletic talent, easily measured, over personality and drive, *and work ethic*, far more difficult to measure.

Not only was Tom Brady, perhaps the NFL's greatest talent overlooked, but Steph Curry was equally disrespected in the NBA draft, based on measurements of physical ability. What was overlooked with both men was the power of personality. Not measured, in any test administered, were will and work ethic. In these measures, both men were second to none.

Bob McKillop shares the following insights about Steph Curry. "He's got a magnetic capacity about him that endears him to teammates, to fans. . . . He makes it so easy to coach him. It seems that every Division I team in America overlooked Curry's drive, work ethic and most of all, personality."

The research of Angela Duckworth that follows suggests that teams are truly mining the wrong data, as her research suggests that natural talent counts and is necessary for success, but effort counts twice as much. The examples of personality trumping inborn talent and gifts extend far beyond athletics, and this chapter will offer a deeper examination to reveal what drove each player to far exceed predictions based on their physical attributes and talents.

THE BIRTH OF *GRIT*: ANGELA DUCKWORTH FINDS HER PASSION

Angela Duckworth, renowned researcher seeking to find what it is that makes one successful in life, developed a psychological test to measure a construct she later labeled *grit*. Her research overwhelmingly documents that what makes us successful in life is not natural talent but *grit*. Grit is the measure of how badly we want a goal (passion) and how much we are willing to persevere or endure to get that goal (perseverance).

Measuring the grit of Tom Brady, Steph Curry, and Michael Jordan would have resulted in scores off the charts. The story of how Duckworth came to this idea of grit is a story that ironically epitomizes the essence of grit. After experimentation with an assortment of career pathways, Angela Duckworth found her true passion in life, not at twenty but as she approached forty.

The exploding field of positive psychology was the forum for that passion, and the research question that drove that passion was the desire to uncover what it is that makes us successful, not only in school but also in life. Duckworth once labeled the first half of her life, in which she dabbled in an assortment of career paths, as lacking grit, "like a boat going from port to port without direction and getting nowhere."

These forays into disparate career explorations were actually a part of the journey to discover her true passion. Sometimes, before we discover our passion, we need to discover what is not our passion. Duckworth's first nearly forty years were part of a search for her *passion*. Once she found that passion, she developed the perseverance to overcome any obstacle.

In discovering her passion, Duckworth brought to life this quote by Les Allen about finding your calling.

> The thing that you do, after your day job, in your free time, too early in the morning, too late at night. That thing that you read about, write about, think about, in fact fanaticize about. That thing that you do when you're all alone and there's no one to impress, nothing to prove, no money to be made, simply a passion to pursue. That's it. That's your thing. That's your heart, your guide. That's the thing that you must, must do.

This passion described above is the reason that sports often gets it so wrong on athletes when they measure only natural talent.

What Duckworth discovered, after being chastised for lacking a clear theory in her second year of study at the University of Pennsylvania, was the awesome power of passion for a goal to inspire effort. Passion and effort are the secret ingredients that make us successful in life. In the measure of passion, unlike combine scores, I am sure that few could rival Tom Brady, Steph Curry, or Michael Jordan.

Duckworth's measurable construct, *grit*, derived from the movie, *True Grit*, proved to be the best predictor of success in a host of eclectic fields. Her new construct measuring both passion for a goal and perseverance to achieve that goal predicted who would stay at West Point through the tortuous first weeks of *Beast Barracks*, win the spelling bee, and remain in teaching after the first five years.

Resilience and perseverance are often inappropriately used as synonyms for grit. The reason that this is a misconception is that this simple definition leaves out resilience and perseverance's most important partner, the secret ingredient that gives rise to persistence and resilience, *passion*.

Passion is the fuel for the perseverance that follows, and without passion, grit is merely dogged persistence. Persistence, not for an immediate, obtainable goal, but for long-term goals, is what creates grit in your life. When you think about successful people, like Abraham Lincoln or Walt Disney, think about the passion for long-term goals that drove these individuals to greatness over the hardships that shaped their lives.

Duckworth's renowned and researched equation for success is: *As much as talent counts, effort counts twice.* Duckworth's theory presents a formula that enables us to better understand the stories of America's most winning coaches and helps to explain how professional sports got it so wrong.

WHAT MAKES GRITTY INDIVIDUALS GRITTY?

The blueprint that Duckworth proposes to explain paragons of grit begins with infatuation. Infatuation might be considered the antecedent of passion, but in this case, the infatuation does not end in a short-term fascination or a fleeting fancy but in a long-term relentless drive. In some of us, the infatuation takes hold and does not let go.

Infatuation gives root to passion, and in gritty individuals, inspires sustained deliberate practice. Deliberate practice is no ordinary practice, but a designed practice in which individuals work specifically with a plan for improvement that is beyond the mere enjoyment of the activity.

Deliberate practice involves working on analyzing and addressing weaknesses, continuous feedback and adjustment based on feedback, and a prolonged effort that is not always enjoyable. It is not the quantity of hours alone that predicts greatness; it is the quality of those hours of practice.

Topping off the pyramid, Duckworth proposes that the individual's infatuation and subsequent deliberate practice culminates in a purpose far greater than the mastery of the task. The final stage in paragons of grit moves the desire for mastery from individual acclaim and mastery to a far greater purpose and meaning.

In some cases, the elevated purpose might be improving the sport itself by developing play to a higher level or in more creative directions than has ever been known. Greater meaning might also mean winning for something greater than yourself, your teammates, your institution or your city.

No one will ever forget Lebron James, collapsed on the basketball court in Cleveland after bringing home a first championship to the city of his birth. When individuals are truly gritty, the end goal does not become merely the celebration of their achievement and acclaim, it has greater purpose than individual accomplishment. It stems from a desire to elevate all to their level.

The reason that movies are made and books are written about individual paragons of grit is because it takes extraordinary belief, effort, and will to achieve this legendary status. Think of Rocky bolstered by a deliberate practice for achieving a goal that he is passionate about and you have the embodiment of grit that Americans have fallen in love with.

The pyramid in figure 4.1 probably does not factor into the thinking of any professional team in making a selection in their draft, but maybe it should.

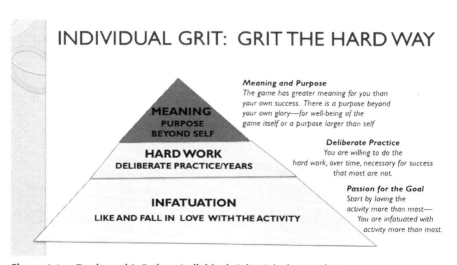

Figure 4.1. Duckworth's Path to Individual Grit: Grit the Hard Way.

This pyramid might be useful in explaining the careers of athletes that defy the statistical measure of their athletic potential.

DRIVEN FROM WITHIN: THE POWER OF EFFORT AND WILL

Certainly one of the most popular Horatio Alger sports legends in America is the rise of Michel Jordan after the initial disappointment of being cut from the varsity. After not making the varsity team in his sophomore season, Jordan was unable to afford a ticket to even see the varsity team play in away games during his junior year.

The only way he could travel with the team was as a statistician. To gain entry to those away games, Jordan carried someone else's jersey past the ticket takers. Those retelling Jordan's story often use this example to condemn the coach for an error in judgment in not selecting one of America's greatest players. However, in his autobiography, *Driven from Within*, Jordan lauds the coach as one of the driving forces behind his success.

This story of Michael Jordan does not condemn his coach; it celebrates that coach's support. But it also provides a window into the nature of gritty individuals. Jordan states in his autobiography, *Driven from Within*,

> I relied on my high school coach, Clifton "Pop" Herring. He picked me up every morning my junior year and took me into the gym before school and worked me out. He was more or less my pusher. He was one of those coaches who just talked to you. . . . He'd pick me up at 6:30. We'd shoot jump shots, play one on one and work on ball handling drills because I couldn't handle the ball at all. We would work for an hour and then I would shower and go to class.

Stories such as Jordan's capture our imaginations and our hearts. Jordan's success in the face of this early rejection has been held up to generations of young people as an example of what anyone can accomplish with effort and will. These stories reveal the power of personality and the magic of passion for a goal, fueling the persistence needed to endure deliberate practice.

In his own words, Jordan shares, the power of passion for a long-term goal.

> I wasn't a great athlete at the time, though I wanted to be. Playing sports was my only way to move up the ladder. It wasn't about fitting in—I wanted to *really* fit in. I wanted to be admired, respected. I wanted the girls to respect me too. I didn't want to just carry their books. All of that drove me more than most people think.

Jordan describes the commitment needed for success: "You have to be uncompromised in your level of commitment, to whatever you are doing, or it can disappear as fast it appeared." Jordan could be the poster child for Duckworth's characterization of gritty individuals and the deliberate practice that transforms their early disappointments.

THE TOM BRADY: THE POWER OF BELIEF AND EFFORT

Tom Brady, whatever your feelings about him, and feelings about Brady tend to generate strong emotional reaction, confirm this assertion that natural or inborn athletic talent might not be the most important factor in predicting quarterback excellence in the NFL. Brady's rise to prominence further substantiates Duckworth's case that belief and effort trump innate natural talent.

Even when drafted later than could be imagined after the success of his senior year at Michigan, although it angered him, Tom Brady never lost belief in his ability. This ability to maintain belief when all others doubted him was the key to his success.

Brady's first meeting with Patriot owner Bob Kraft epitomizes how unshakable was Tom Brady's belief in himself. When Brady ran into the Patriot's owner at training camp after the draft, he is reported to have said, "Mr. Kraft, I'm Tom Brady, you don't know me. But I am the best decision that this franchise has ever made." The confidence embodied in that statement after such a disappointing draft selection helps to explain Tom Brady's success.

The story of unshakable belief has truly deep implications for anyone that has ever been underestimated or overlooked based on natural talent. Our knowledge of Brady's remarkable success presents a clear argument that grit does not arrive supernaturally, out of thin air, but is built on belief.

Brady first needed to possess the belief that effort was the key to success and not natural athletic ability. Without this core belief in place, Brady would be watching football today and not playing it. The combination of knowing what to do to achieve his goals and having the will to do what needed to be done in the face of obstacles that might deter others is at the heart of Brady's success.

When his hope was tested, when his ability was doubted, when others might have quit, it was Brady's unshakeable hold on belief that kept him going. Tom's most recent revelation about his 8:30 p.m. bedtime in *Business Insider* is a clear indicator that his level of passion has not diminished. "Strength training and conditioning and how I really treat my body are important to me, because there is really *nothing else that I enjoy like playing football*, I want to do this as long as I can."

In the *TB12 Method*, Brady lays out a rigorous program in which all of his decisions center on performance enhancement. Putting in the effort beyond comprehension, facing down the critics and disappointments, constantly climbing back up after getting knocked down, can only be fueled by a passion for a goal that is so great that an individual perseveres when others would not.

What all of us need to keep in mind is that this is not a magical power endowed from above, but strength built on belief and effort. The other candidates that you did not eliminate in our NFL draft elimination exercise became pretty good quarterbacks in their own right. You can check in appendix A at the back of the book to see which quarterback you would have selected with your first pick as a general manager in the draft exercise.

The purpose of the exercise should reveal to you that the unmeasured characteristics of passion for the goal, driven by belief and effort, can be even more important than any statistic.

RÉSUMÉ VERSUS EULOGY VIRTUES

The lesson of Tom Brady should make you think the candidate's time in the forty-yard dash might not be the best predictor of NFL success. Stronger predictors might be a candidate's scores on tests measuring belief and effort. On those tests, Tom Brady would have no peer. Why this matters is that the research and the examples that have been presented make the case that we should consider personality at least as much as we consider natural talent in building our organizations.

Pete Carroll and Angela Duckworth in their collaboration of science and sport discuss the fact that teams need players with not just résumé virtues, athletic accomplishments, but character virtues, or eulogy virtues—that is, things that people want to be remembered for after they die. These characteristics of integrity, honesty, and perseverance define the teams that play Springfield volleyball and all teams that win consistently.

Striving is what competing is all about—striving for excellence, striving for knowledge. It has nothing to do with winning or losing. It is about a mentality and a mindset that gives us direction in creating a culture. This key to building any culture is getting the right people on the bus, people, who will buy into that striving.

Watching one opposing team, I suggested to Coach Sullivan that this dominant player on the other team would have made his team unbeatable on any level. I was shocked when the coach's response was that the player had wanted to come to Springfield, but Springfield did not want him as a player.

Coach Sullivan's brief response was that his character would never have fit into our culture and had the potential to destroy that culture.

In our trophy culture, in which general managers seek to buy championships on the open market, it is rare to find those willing to make their choices based on character and personality. Every step of the climb to success for a great athlete has been built on individual accomplishment. It is difficult enough to find those athletes who are gifted athletically, but it nearly impossible to discover individuals who have achieved that level of acclaim and are more selfless than selfish.

This does not mean that these individuals come ready packaged with these values intact and ready for consumption. Culture is learned and there is no exception in sports. Players have missteps along the way. Coaches do not select players perfect in these core values, but rather those capable of learning them. Coach Sullivan likes to say, "Not everyone is capable or willing to get on your bus."

One team that has captured the imagination of the nation and built a culture by factoring in character to its decision-making process is the Chicago Cubs. In Tom Verducci's book *The Cubs Way*, Cubs General Manager Theo Epstein explains the Cubs' meteoric rise to championship as accomplished by focusing on character:

> If we can't find the next technological breakthrough, maybe we can be better than anyone else in how we treat our players and how we connect with players and the relationships we develop and how we put them in positions to succeed. Maybe our environment will be the best in the game, maybe our vibe will be the best in the game, maybe our players will be the loosest in the game, and maybe they will have the most fun and maybe they will care the most. It is impossible to quantify.

It is easy to see the journey that Theo Epstein had to take in replacing his faith in the numbers that define baseball statistics with character. In 2011, Theo had seen Boston's lead slip away with a toxic climate in which players not only feuded, but one player was even heard to question why they should want to play in October since they were not paid for those days. At this point, Theo Epstein concluded that he had talented players with losing attitudes.

What transformed the Chicago Cubs was not an abandonment of statistics, but an enhancement of those strategies by injecting character into the search for players. Players with high character were sought after and the questions that were involved in drafting the team expanded to how the player handled adversity and how they conducted their lives.

The statement above certainly is reflective of the formula that Charlie Sullivan has established at Springfield College. The same core values that defined their success can define yours if you factor the power of personality into your personnel selections.

Five Takeaways from *The Power of Personality*

1. Grit, the passion and perseverance for the long term goals is a researched construct that has been proven in numerous studies to predict success over natural talent alone.
2. The preoccupation of sports teams to evaluate and value innate athletic talent over personality traits has led to teams missing out on extraordinary individuals with hidden potential to lead their organizations to success.
3. Belief and work ethic are the driving forces that spell success in life. Grit research has demonstrated that natural talent is often inversely correlated with grit. The most talented can often be the least gritty individuals.
4. Gritty individuals first possess a natural infatuation for an activity and are then defined by a willingness to do the deliberate practice that makes them successful. Finally, these individuals are marked by a drive for greater purpose and meaning than individual success.
5. The power of personality, in the words of Duckworth, is that, *As much as talent counts, effort counts twice.*

The Big Idea from *The Power of Personality*

Winning leaders need to select individuals for their organizations on more than natural talent. Successful organizations need to measure the personality traits of the individual and gauge belief, effort, and will in the individual, if they want to build championship organizations.

II

BUILDING CULTURAL GRIT

Failing Well and Core Beliefs

It's okay to be discouraged. It's not okay to quit. To know you want to quit but plant your feet and keep inching forward until you take the impenetrable fortress you've decided to lay siege to in your own life— that's persistence.

—Ryan Holiday

It's not hard not to make decisions when you know what your values are.

—Roy Disney

Your core values are the commonly held beliefs that authentically define your soul.

—John Maxwell

TRIAL BY FIRE: CORE VALUES BORN OF STRUGGLE, FRUSTRATION, AND FAILURE

Failure is never a pleasant experience, most often, it is a low point, but it can also be a turning point. After being fired by both the Patriots and by the Jets, Pete Carroll was at that low point. In fact, that firing may have been the lowest point in his career.

With every setback comes an opportunity that may at first go unnoticed in the emotion of disappointment that surrounds us. For Pete Carroll, his last firing by New England gave him to time to reinvent himself. Reading and reflecting are luxuries that one does not often have as a head football coach in the NFL. His reading drew him back to his inspiration and role model in coaching, John Wooden.

After an in-depth study on John Wooden's carefully constructed *Pyramid of Success*, Pete Carroll realized, not only did he not have a model of his beliefs, but *he also had never defined and spelled out exactly what he believed were the keys to success.* If he was not clear on what he believed, how could his teams know and actualize those beliefs. If this is your case, you are piloting a ship without a clear destination.

Wooden had also arrived at his insights after a period of struggle and frustration. After fifteen years as a high school English teacher and basketball coach, he had become exasperated by the typical parents' definition of success as an "A" or a win in basketball, Wooden developed a pyramid of success that defined success beyond A's and winning.

Wooden's pyramid of success was about the character traits that would translate to winning in life, after the basketball court. Wooden's pyramid focused on the transformation of individuals in the process of seeking excellence, rather than the trophies or acclaim that resulted from that process. His pyramid shared a set of core values and the way that he expected his teams to play *and to conduct their lives.*

Although Wooden's teams did not dominate the national basketball world for the next fifteen years after he instituted his values, his teams remained true to those core beliefs. In 1960, all of that changed as his teams went on to win ten of the next eleven national championships, a record that may never be matched again. More importantly, as a coach and teacher, he had impacted the lives of his players winning those championships far beyond their playing days.

Wooden developed a philosophy that sought goals that teach individuals to strive to become the best people that they possibly can, both on and *off the court.* Without ever actually mentioning winning, Wooden created the most winning culture in the history of American basketball. Listen below as Coach Wooden elaborates on the role of character in the success of a team.

Figure 5.1.   John Wooden's Talks About the Pyramid of Success, https://www.youtube.com/watch?v=vi-2E6BPfgk. Author created.

Pete Carroll's realization that he lacked a set of beliefs uses Wooden's philosophical pyramid as the lighthouse for redefining his life and his coaching. Reflecting on his own life and character, he defined his beliefs and the values responsible for the successes that he had enjoyed in coaching individuals and teams throughout his career.

Unlike Wooden's time, our era often shares deep meaning in memes, sound bites, and Twitter posts. For this reason, Carroll often translates his core values with three simple rules rather than the extensive hierarchy spelled out in Wooden's pyramid. The brilliance of this simplicity is that these simple phrases have become the common language of his culture. *Always compete, no excuses*, and *be on time* are the phrases that define Pete Carroll's core beliefs and now define every action of his Seattle Seahawk organization, for both players and coaches.

Although those simple terms may seem simplistic at first, they have deep meaning for all in the organization. *Always compete* does not mean what it appears to signify at first glance. Rather than competing solely against opponents, players soon learn that each player is competing against himself in a struggle to become the best player, *and person*, they can be. Carroll emphasizes that the greatness of the opponent is what brings out even greater levels of excellence in each of us.

The Seahawks compete and strive together to be the best they can be in every drill and challenge they face. This idea of striving to be the best player has focused Carroll's practices on competition. On "Competition Wednesdays," players compete against one another to earn or hold positions. Rather than seeing the man across line as an enemy, Carroll urges his players to see their competitor as the source of their greatness.

The second core value, *no excuses*, relates to the fact that players will not make excuses after setbacks, but rather learn from failures to become even stronger. Making excuses or assigning blame will not help players get better, while accepting responsibility for setbacks enables the player and the team to continually grow.

When Carroll's controversial decision to throw on the goal line resulted in a disastrous loss in the 2015 Super Bowl, he was asked how the team got past that loss; his response, "*We* will use it," brings to life the team's core values. This idea that mistakes can make us better has made his teams accountable for errors, seeking only to grow from errors in their quest to be the best team that they can be.

Finally, the value, *be on time*, which has really been modified to mean *be early*, makes concrete the belief that respect for the team and for team rules must be greater than individual concerns or needs. In addition, this value demands players be organized and manage time well, a basic operating principle for the entire organization. To be late is to show disrespect for the team and a lack of organization.

Protect the Team, embodies the overall philosophy that ties all three values together. Pete Carroll demands players use these actual phrases in the camp, on the field, and in their lives—*no synonyms*. Using these exact phrases offers proof that the core beliefs are internalized in each player, but it also demonstrates that these core values are lived and reinforced.

Carroll ends his book *Win Forever* by asking the United States Commander of Special Forces to define the core values that define America's elite fighting forces in twenty-five words or less. When the commander stumblingly recognizes that he cannot articulate his beliefs the way that Carroll has, he responds that he has homework to do. Do you have homework to do as a coach, leader, or *teacher*? Could you articulate your core values in twenty-five words?

The lesson for all of us is that leaders need to carefully define and spell out their beliefs if they expect their organization to put those values into play. More importantly, leaders of organizations need to live out those core values in every decision they make and every action they take. Leaders need to publish and reinforce their core beliefs if they expect their organizations to reflect those values.

Pete Carroll is fond of challenging leaders in all arenas of life to present to him their core philosophy in twenty-five words or less. That is the challenge presented to you the reader. Take the time that Pete Carroll did to clearly map out and write down what your core values are and how you define each of the principles in practice. For a view of the core values that are defined by Charles Sullivan to be the lighthouse for his team, refer to appendix C.

WINNING COACHES AND CORE VALUES

Coaches who win all the time differ in sport, personality, and—at first glance—nearly everything. What they do not differ in is that they all have a clear core of values from which every decision and action of the team is derived. When you strip away the obvious differences, it is striking how similar their essential core beliefs are to each other.

What is even more striking is that core values do not come easily to winners. Core values tend to emerge after our greatest struggles, frustrations, and even failures. What defines core beliefs defines the character of the people who make up their teams and the vision of how those people will function as a team on and beyond the playing fields.

FAILING WELL: THE SECRET OF SUCCESS IN LIFE

What might be comforting to you is that America's most successful coaches did not usually arrive at the top of their fields without first overcoming devastating failure. What is common to all of these coaches and to all who successfully overcome obstacles is that they all *failed well.*

Failing well means that individuals not only survive failures but thrive as a result of unexpected insights and directions that emerge from those things that don't work out. Failure is viewed as a stepping-stone to success, and not an indictment of their ability.

This ability to grow from defeat and learn from mistakes, rather than believe that your lack of success is the result of a lack of inborn capacity, is the life's work of researcher Carol Dweck. After a lifetime of research, Dweck concluded that individuals generally believe that success is either *fixed*—that is, derived from inborn *capacity*—or is *incremental*, more determined by *effort*. Those who believe that their success is directly and profoundly linked to their effort and that skill increases with more effort are said to have *a growth mindset.*

The research does not clearly determine whether success is more related to capacity or effort, but it does predict how our *thinking* about those beliefs will affect success in life. Those with a growth mindset, believing success is based on effort, continue to grow and achieve higher levels of accomplishment as life goes on. Those with a fixed mindset, believing success is based on inborn talent, tend to plateau early in life and not grow beyond this point.

Dweck's groundbreaking research is shared in the best seller, *Mindset: The New Psychology of Success*, and this resource should be required reading for any of us who believe that we are doomed by a lack of natural talent. The research on mindset is the latest rage in education, but it is applicable in every arena of life.

There are no better examples of growth mindset success than the lives of the extraordinary coaches referenced in this text, who provide clear exemplars for Dweck's growth mindset research. The core values of each coach are not only marked by early setbacks, but are also forged by those setbacks. Without an ability to fail well, these coaches may have ended up in other lines of work.

Five Takeaways from *Failing Well and Core Values*

1. Coaches, teams, and organizations will experience failure, frustration, and disappointment. A growth mindset understands that these setbacks can actually make us stronger and point out the directions that we must take for success.
2. What great leaders share is the ability to fail well and turn obstacles and setbacks into opportunities.
3. Organizations and teams that consistently win operate under core values that drive every situation and decision. An organization without defined core values is like a ship without a rudder.

4. Although each of the winning coaches in this text are markedly different, what they have in common is that they have arrived at a set of core
values that are more similar than different.

5. Iconic coaches and businesses leaders do not just identify and post their
core values on a bulletin board; they live those core values on a daily
basis. Creating a written philosophy of core values not only reduces the
uncertainty and anxiety of every decision, but also makes every decision one that is consistent.

The Big Idea from *Failing Well and Core Values*

What all great leaders define for their organizations is a set of clearly articulated core values that drive every decision and action of the organization.
These core values are often born of previous failures and setbacks by the
leader. The struggles and life lessons make the core values more than words
on paper.

6

Cultural Grit

If you want to be grittier, find a gritty culture and join it. If you're a leader and you want the people in your organization to be grittier, create a gritty culture.

—Angela Lee Duckworth

Leadership is the energetic process of getting people fully and willingly committed to a new and sustainable course of action, to meet commonly agreed upon objectives whilst having commonly held values.

—Mick Yates

You walk in there, and you're like, "Oh, this is a culture. I get it. . . ." People have an identity there that they feel special.

—Angela Duckworth on Seattle Seahawks Culture

THE UNEXPECTED PHONE CALL: SCIENCE MEETS SPORT

Whenever the phone rings and we are not sure who is on the other end or what the subject of that call is, our hearts tend to beat a stroke or two faster. Although an unexpected call can be jolting, it can also lead to new connections. Angela Duckworth, the renowned grit researcher, received this kind of late-night phone call from Pete Carroll, coach of the Seattle Seahawks football team.

As famous as the name Pete Carroll would be to most Americans, not being a football fan, Duckworth was unfamiliar with both Carroll and his team, the Seattle Seahawks. That phone call began a collision of science and sport that was revealing for each and set in motion the concept of cultural grit.

Before we get ahead of ourselves, let's retrace the roots of that call. Angela Duckworth had recently rocked the world of applied positive psychology with her research findings on grit. In sharing that research, grit was revealed in several trending TED Talks to be a key factor in success in teaching, surviving the challenging initiation at West Point, the National Spelling Bee, and achievement in a host of other arenas.

In her legendary six-minute TED talk in May 2013, Duckworth had captured the attention of Pete Carroll. The Seahawks football coach was riveted to her every word until the very end of that talk. The research on grit had struck a powerful chord in Carroll, but Duckworth's concluding thought jarred him and motivated him to contact Dr. Duckworth immediately.

Ending her talk from a purely scientific perspective, Duckworth concluded with the scientific observation that we are not sure how to develop grit or even if we can increase grit. Attempting to inspire more research on developing grit in individuals, Duckworth ends the talk with a call to arms, a rather dramatic plea for more research.

> We need to take our best ideas, our strongest intuitions, and we need to test them. We need to measure whether we have been successful and we need to be willing to fail, to be wrong, to start over again. In other words, we need to get "gritty" to get our kids grittier.

What was being shared was Duckworth's assertion that scientists had not definitively proven that grit could be purposefully increased through designed interventions. Intrigued and excited about the research on grit, Carroll was stunned by the claim suggesting that we do not know if we have the ability to develop grit in individuals.

Although Duckworth was viewing this ability from a purely scientific perspective, Carroll responded from his perspective as a coach, believing that he had spent his entire life creating a *culture* that successfully fostered *grit*, a *cultural grit* that defined his teams. This phone call had profound and far-reaching implications for both parties. After that phone call, the worlds of science and sport collided.

Use the QR code below to hear Duckworth's famous TED talk and her call to arms for more research at the end that so dramatically captured Carroll's attention.

Figure 6.1. Angela Duckworth's TED Talk: Getting Gritty About Passion and Perseverance. Author created.

The deep relationship that developed as a result of this phone call led to a more extensive examination of the idea of grit as an outgrowth of culture. Investigating Carroll's claim that the goal of his coaching was to create a culture of grit, Duckworth visited the Seahawks' training facility to experience firsthand this validity of growing grit in individuals as a designed outcome of culture. *That*, as they say in the movie, *Casablanca, was the beginning of beautiful friendship.*

This relationship between Carroll and Duckworth became more than a mutual admiration society; it became an avenue of growth for both parties. The exploration of cultural grit from both athletic and scientific perspectives was the impetus for this book. Duckworth's immersion into Seahawk culture had a profound effect on her thinking and research, in turn inspiring this study of winning coaches.

The interview, linked to the QR code below, shares a town hall meeting exchange between Duckworth and Carroll on the topic of whether a culture can grow or foster grit in an individual. Indeed, as Duckworth contends in the interview, *science went to school on sport.*

Figure 6.2. Angela Duckworth and Pete Carroll on Cultural Grit. Author created.

What Duckworth observes firsthand at the Seahawks Camp is that the team does in fact have a unique culture, and the power of conforming to that culture seems to cultivate and nurture grit. In her groundbreaking best seller, *Grit: The Power of Passion and Perseverance*, Duckworth concludes the book with a deep analysis of grit as a function of culture.

At the Seahawks' training camp, Duckworth feels the culture in every meeting with the team, she hears it in chants of the players, who echo the exact phrases that define the culture. Her conversations with players confirm her feeling that the core values of the culture are internalized in each player, nurturing passion and perseverance for long-term goals.

Applying the research of sociologist Don Chambliss to analyze the phenomenon of the grit of an organization, Duckworth adapts her research beyond the study of grit solely as an individually developed character trait and focuses on grit as a quality that can be fostered by an organization. Chambliss had suggested the easiest way to become a great swimmer is to join a great swim team.

His assertion is counterintuitive to the popular belief that great swimmers make a great team and introduces the notion that it is great teams that make great swimmers. Exploring the power of conformity and applying the work of social scientists in the field, Duckworth captures the essence of this research, concluding, "If you want to be grittier, find a gritty culture and join it. If you're a leader and you want the people in your organization to be grittier, create a gritty culture."

Duckworth makes the case that human behavior conforms to the norms of the group and that culture defines our identity. The real power that leaders have is the power to create a culture of grit. Building on this partnership of science and sport, what is proposed is that Charlie Sullivan and coaches who win all the time, develop and nurture cultural grit in the members of the culture.

Winning cultures inspire a unique identity in the members of their team. This group identity drives behavior in ways motivated beyond individual gain. *Cultural grit* is a term that we will employ to discuss this phenomenon of the power of a culture to inspire grit in its members.

MAKING THE CASE FOR CULTURAL GRIT

The reason that movies are made and books are written about individual paragons of grit is because it takes extraordinary belief, effort, and will to achieve this legendary status on your own. What makes the stories of these cultural heroes embodying grit so moving is that their accomplishments seem unattainable to most of us. The fact that accomplishments appear beyond our reach makes for an exciting book or movie, but does not provide much of a model to emulate.

The underlying message in our most inspiring movies is that characters like Rocky Balboa or Rudy possess an almost supernatural drive. These larger-than-life individuals are presented as super heroes, rather than as *gritty* people possessing such a strong *passion* for their goals that they are willing to *persevere* when others are not. That representation would make for a less entertaining movie, but might be more inspiring to those of us struggling against overwhelming odds.

Chambliss's study of Olympic swimmers supported the idea that grit is more attainable as a cultural phenomenon than an individual struggle. Chambliss proposes, "there is a hard way to get grit and an easy way. The hard way is to do it by yourself. The easy way is to use conformity—the basic human drive to fit in—because if you are around a lot of people who are gritty, you are going to be gritty."

When one examines the record of Charlie Sullivan and compares his success to the legendary coaches cross-referenced, the idea of growing grit through culture emerges powerfully. Closer examination of the practices and core values of these iconic coaches reveals not how different each of these cultures is, but how similar.

What becomes clear in dissecting the similar patterns present in winning programs is that coaching success is deeply rooted in psychological and sociological research and is driven by a remarkably similar foundation. The science that is emerging on goal motivation and grit are offering researched evidence on why some teams win consistently and other teams struggle in mediocrity.

THE CULTURAL GRIT PYRAMID

This foundation for cultural grit is more easily presented in a schematic than in words alone. Although every coach referenced differs in temperament, personality, and methods, what unites these great leaders is that their cultures are defined by three basic tenets. To make the similarities between these disparate coaches more discernable, we have represented the shared core values in a diagram consisting of three levels.

The Cultural Grit Pyramid is derived from analyzing the core values of coaches who win *all the time*. Although each of these coaches is strikingly different, deeper scrutiny reveals that despite the differences in approach or manner, the core values that define each coach are strikingly similar and can be represented by the levels of the pyramid.

LEVEL ONE: SHARED EFFORT AND BELIEF

The Cultural Grit Pyramid builds its base on the power of conformity. There is a distinct culture in place and individuals immediately get a sense that there is a definitive set of core beliefs and "ways that things that are done around here" defined by the culture. These beliefs are not just implied, but are often written down and are constantly reinforced.

The core values have been developed by a trial-and-error process by the coach, *and are clearly represented* by every individual in the organization. When Bill Belichick was asked how he gets along with his younger more modern players, he responded that the main goal and the driving force in his life is football. If it is not the main goal in their lives, they will not be around very long.

The established core values nurture skills and dispositions that extend beyond playing fields. The core values drive every action and decision and are lived by the players, the coach, and the organization. Adherence to these core values is reinforced by the belief of the group members in the leader and his every action.

Many leaders and coaches post a list of core values at the beginning of a season, and this is basically the agenda of the opening meeting and often ignored as the season goes on. On less effective teams, players know that the core values will be abandoned shortly after that first meeting and the initial posting on the bulletin board is merely a meeting that they have to endure.

Coaches who win all the time function with these core values serving as the operating procedures of the organization. Individuals and situations can often test the core values of the culture, but great leaders defend the core values, even when that defense comes at the expense of individuals. No individual is greater than the core values of the team. New players sense and can feel the core values and the difference between this team and others they may have played on.

The base of the pyramid in gritty cultures is characterized by a shared belief between the coach and the player that arises from relentless effort. The culture demands relentless effort on the part of both parties. The coach's work ethic and knowledge of the game in gritty cultures is unparalleled and often inspirational. The coach lives this work ethic in order to serve as an example of the expected behavior for all.

The result of the effort of the coach is a belief by the team that the coach's effort and insight will result in their becoming superior players and being successful as a team. Without this belief in the coach, the players will not deliver the relentless work ethic needed for mastery of process.

The belief between the coach and the players must be a two-way street. The coach must also believe in the player's abilities and level of effort. The shared effort and belief form the base of the Cultural Grit Pyramid.

The mutual values of shared effort and belief, not only affect player's success as athletes, but their success as people, beyond the field. Players come to realize that this same level of effort is required in life beyond the field. There is a sense in players in successful organizations that their effort is about more than winning and losing; it is transformative to who they are as people.

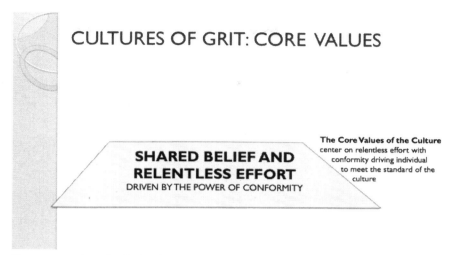

CULTURES OF GRIT: CORE VALUES

SHARED BELIEF AND RELENTLESS EFFORT

DRIVEN BY THE POWER OF CONFORMITY

The Core Values of the Culture center on relentless effort with conformity driving individual to meet the standard of the culture

Figure 6.3. Shared Belief and Relentless Effort: The Foundation of Cultural Grit. Author created.

The mutual belief shared by the coach and players creates a culture that can be immediately felt by new members joining the team. The power of conformity instills the relentless effort needed for the deliberate practice that defines cultural grit and this becomes the signature value of team.

LEVEL TWO: STRIVING FOR PERFECTION IN PROCESS

The second level of the pyramid involves a focus on developing perfect fundamentals, driven by a process-over-product orientation. Legendary coaches are dedicated to a focus on process and are unaffected by the short-term product, the score in a given game.

Coach Sullivan likes to urge his teams to "*focus on the roots of our program, the process, and not the fruits of our program, the results.*" If the roots are strong, the fruits will emerge naturally. Focusing only on the fruits will result in flowers and fruits that never bloom. This process focus enables players to stay the course whether they are behind or ahead in a contest.

Focusing on process enables the members of the team to stay committed, not just for a game, but over the course of a season. This process focus also results in superior execution of strategy by the team. Winning, *the product*, takes care of itself without the team ever focusing on winning as the goal.

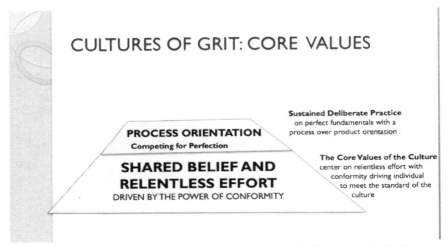

CULTURES OF GRIT: CORE VALUES

PROCESS ORIENTATION
Competing for Perfection

**SHARED BELIEF AND
RELENTLESS EFFORT**
DRIVEN BY THE POWER OF CONFORMITY

Sustained Deliberate Practice
on perfect fundamentals with a
process over product orentation .

The Core Values of the Culture
center on relentless effort with
conformity driving individual
to meet the standard of the
culture

Figure 6.4. The Second Level of the Grit Pyramid: Striving for Perfection in Process.
Author created.

The drive for perfection in process is not merely an individual endeavor by certain members of the team, but a process shared by every member of the team. The mantra of competition is at the heart of Pete Carroll's philosophy, *Always Compete*, as it is in John Wooden's pyramid of success. The perfect process is not only about each individual taking on the challenge to dominate the opponent, but also about a desire to attain the best self one can be.

LEVEL THREE: IDENTITY AND MEANING

The apex of the pyramid is a meaning and purpose that motivates players beyond personal goals and success. Cultural grit forges an identity in team members beyond personal gain. This is a startling consequence, as players have needed to focus on personal goals to attain the individual success needed to earn a place on these types of teams.

What earns players a spot on these professional or collegiate teams is a lifetime of focus on personal success. But on teams that win consistently, players believe that they are part of something bigger than their individual goals and successes. Team identity becomes more powerful for members on winning teams than individual achievement.

This identity as a team member defines the athlete's character beyond a career in a sport. Traditionally, we all work hard for individual gain, but great teams shift the source of that motivation to goals beyond those of individual gain. Great teams are driven by a greater purpose, the success of the team.

Members of the Springfield College Volleyball team know that they are part of something special that goes beyond winning. Members of the New England Patriots, University of Connecticut women's basketball team, John Wooden's UCLA championship teams, and the University of North Carolina soccer teams all experienced this same team identification, defining not only their tremendous careers, *but the rest of their lives.*

This identity-driven motivation empowers coaches with weapons competing coaches often lack. Players on teams defined by cultural grit are willing to sacrifice individual gain for the sake of the team. What is proposed is that coaches who win all the time, despite being different in so many ways, share the core of values on which this Cultural Grit Pyramid has been constructed.

The set of shared values and principles in this pyramid are the determinants of coaching success that extend beyond individual seasons. The core values of cultural grit are life changing as players realize that they are part of something special that will define the rest of their lives.

The Cultural Grit Pyramid has implications far beyond the world of athletics. The real challenge faced in leadership is to build a culture that will nurture that grit, rather than simply imploring each person to be grittier. In education, schools regularly clamor for academic grit without creating a *culture* that nurtures that quality.

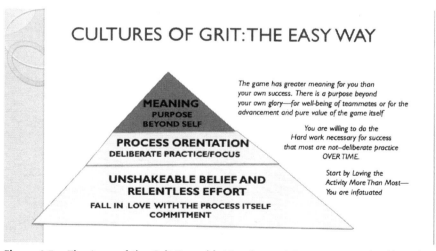

CULTURES OF GRIT: THE EASY WAY

MEANING
PURPOSE
BEYOND SELF

The game has greater meaning for you than your own success. There is a purpose beyond your own glory—for well-being of teammates or for the advancement and pure value of the game itself

PROCESS ORENTATION
DELIBERATE PRACTICE/FOCUS

You are willing to do the Hard work necessary for success that most are not–deliberate practice OVER TIME.

UNSHAKEABLE BELIEF AND
RELENTLESS EFFORT

FALL IN LOVE WITH THE PROCESS ITSELF
COMMITMENT

Start by Loving the Activity More Than Most—You are infatuated

Figure 6.5.   The Apex of the Grit Pyramid: Meaning and Purpose Beyond Self. Author created.

Gritty cultures are the product of a shared belief of the individuals in the leader and the culture, a product-over-process orientation, and an identity with the culture that supplants the needs of the individual. Gritty cultures are transformative for their members, who are actualized as human beings as a result of being part of the culture.

Five Takeaways from *Cultural Grit*

1. The hard way to achieve grit is as an individual on your own. The easy way to become gritty is to join a culture that nurtures grit.
2. Cultures can nurture grit in individuals when built on clear, lived core values. Gritty cultures are transformative for their members, who are actualized as a result of being part of the culture.
3. Gritty cultures are fueled by a belief in the organization and the leader. This belief is a two-way street.
4. Gritty cultures focus on process over result or product, seeking to do things perfectly.
5. Gritty individuals who reach the zenith of their field are generally driven by a purpose that is greater than individual glory. These individuals find meaning in the goals of the team rather than simply individual gain.

The Big Idea from *Cultural Grit*

Gritty cultures share core values that nurture grit. These cultures are defined by a shared belief and effort on the part of the individuals that make up the culture, a focus on product-over-process orientation, and an identity with the culture, making team goals more important than individual goals.

7

Belief

The most important factor in success is mindset. It is how you think. It is the vision you have about what you have to accomplish.

—Nick Saban, Alabama Football Coach

Success is an attitude, a mindset, a decision, a commitment, a promise. A belief that it can be done, should be done, and WILL be done.

—George Akomas Jr.

In coaching, it's important to have a really strong technical basis where you are applying science the right way. You're using rotational analysis. You're using video analysis. You're effective at teaching motor skill. You're not going to take the team's talent to its potential without a really strong technical approach. That's everything from match-day tactics to the preparation of the team. We are sick around here about capturing data.

—Jack Clark, University of California at Berkeley, Rugby Coach

MORE THAN PEP TALKS: BELIEF
BORN OF CONSISTENT EFFORT

As magical and inspiring as Coach Sullivan's speech was to the lacrosse team and other teams before the NCAA opening rounds, we all know in our hearts that the effects of a pregame talk will not sustain a culture of belief *over time*. If you carefully analyze the success of Springfield College Volleyball, it becomes obvious that consistent belief is not built on a single pregame talk, but on the foundation of practices of the team.

The first and most essential of those blocks is an unrelenting and unyielding effort on the part of the coach *and the team.* The culture of belief must also be grounded in the trust that the coach's efforts have produced specific insights that almost guarantee victory and, at the same time, bring out the best in each individual team member. Belief does not come with the title *coach*, but has to be earned. Belief in a coach arises when the coach's demonstrated efforts have produced those insights that have resulted in success time after time. The coach may struggle at the dawn of his or her career, but over time, those struggles need to have produced a formula for success. Effort alone will not result in belief unless it is accompanied by success.

Belief is born of the result of the unmatched effort on the part of the leader or coach to truly uncover the keys to success in their field. What every successful organization possesses is a coach or leader, who establishes belief through a culture built on effort and reflected in the success of the organization.

On the eve of the 2018 NCAA Volleyball Championships, after a truly impressive semifinal victory, texts from Coach Sullivan implied to me that he had a feeling that not everyone embraced the belief that previous championship teams had exhibited. Not many coaches would have been able to read and sense this mood of their team after such an impressive semifinal performance.

Great coaches have this sixth sense, and Coach Sullivan's intuition told him that not everyone in the locker room was winning their individual game of belief. What followed for Coach Sullivan was a night of film study that went deep into the night, ending just before dawn. After getting only three hours of sleep, Coach Sullivan's next text to me simply read, *I got it.*

Coach Sullivan had identified on the films three sets that he believed the opponent simply could not defend. What is significant is that his team also adopted the belief that their opponent could not defend these sets. The result of this all-night effort by the coach and the belief instilled in his team was another NCAA championship.

What most outsiders to the team will never know is that this victory was built on the effort of the coach, insights from data, and the matching belief of the players in the coach and their game plan. To the spectators, the victory was just another victory, easily attributed to the superiority of Springfield's players and not this kind of effort on the part of the coach.

No player would consider not giving the supreme effort for a coach who forsakes his sleep to empower his team with the insights on an opponent that could almost guarantee victory. Whether Coach Sullivan's strategic adjustments had made the team invincible or whether the team *believed* that the adjustments had made the team invincible is a matter for debate. What is not up for debate is that truly winning coaches all inspire this same level of belief in their leadership and direction.

Although consistently winning coaches go down different paths on the road to success, all arrive at the same point. What is striking is that each coach became stronger and grew after defeats that led to reflection and deeper insights into the game. The philosophies that arose are strikingly similar. All coaches at the top levels of their sport have inspired belief that begins with an unsurpassed work ethic.

Bill Belichick learned the secret of effort as the foundation for belief from his father, Steve Belichick, an assistant football coach at Navy. Bill had accumulated an unparalleled collection of football strategy and knowledge from his father's tutelage and collection of football books. This foundation of knowledge, however, was just the beginning for Belichick. What makes Belichick extraordinary is that his foundation of insights never stops growing, because he has a work ethic second to none. Belichick has stated that he never watches a football game at any level without adding to his base of knowledge.

Some Patriots may work out or prepare for an opponent on film in the facility until long after midnight, others may arrive at 5 a.m. There is one constant, no matter when the workout time, early or late, Belichick can be found in the building. Rumors that Coach Belichick sleeps in Gillette Stadium on many nights are more than rumors.

When the Patriots miraculously beat the San Francisco 49ers by intercepting a pass on the one-yard line with time running out, Coach Pete Carroll was crucified for making the worst call in the history of the league. Defending Carroll, some have debated whether it was the fault of the play call or the failure of the players to execute it. What most failed to see was that the Patriot's success in the waning moments of that Super Bowl was built on the attention to detail of the coach.

In diagnosing every possible situation and preparing his team to meet the challenge of every situation, Belichick had predicted that this unique passing play could be run in goal-line situations. The Patriots had practiced and rerun this same play over and over. Data analysis had revealed this particular play to be one of the Seahawk's favorite plays in goal-line situations.

Malcolm Butler, the defensive back covering the receiver, had been unsuccessful in defending the play in practice. Coach Belichick was all over Malcolm after several unsuccessful attempts to stop the play during practice. Belichick insisted that Malcolm had to be able to make that play. Due to prodding of Coach Belichick, Malcolm became prepared and ready to make that play when it counted. The rest is history. Malcolm intercepted the goal-line pass and the Patriots had another Super Bowl ring.

Opinions are divided on whether blame should be cast on Pete Carroll for the call or credit awarded to Malcolm Butler for making a spectacular interception. Few have looked deeply enough to discover that the seeds of victory were actually sown in the extreme attention to detail and meticulous planning of Coach Belichick. Successes, born of attention to detail and insight, inspire a belief in the coach and his directions that lives on long after the play is in the books.

BELIEF AND EFFORT: A TWO-WAY STREET

In building a culture of belief, the work effort of the coach is so remarkable that players joining any of these legendary teams know immediately that there is something special about this team. Any player recruited by or traded to one of these dynastic teams is struck by the effort and preparation of the coach, which filters down to every member of the organization.

Coaches, who win all the time, are meticulous in preparation and players immediately sense that the coach's efforts are not only profound, but have unlocked secrets of the game that have the power to transform their level of play. The power of conformity is strong, and it is not conceivable that anyone joining a team with a coach who works this hard in preparation and to this degree would give less of an effort than the coach.

Top NFL agent, Peter Schaeffer maintains that when Belichick tells a player to open his stance six inches more, his coaching is immediately put into practice by the player. The reason for this is not simply compliance, but the belief that the insights of this coach will result in improved personal performance. This type of commitment is not awarded to every coach, but is earned by those coaches who win all the time.

Should there be player, who does not conform to the values of the team, they are not long for the organization. The Patriots have made a history of trading top performers who do not meet the standard of the team. Belief is born of a respect for the effort of the coach, and the culture that emerges is one built on the team's relentless effort in pursuit of perfection.

Players on teams that win all the time come to believe that the coach's effort will result in victory, but there is sometime even more at play. They believe that the effort they give will be transformative for them as individuals.

DATA-DRIVEN CULTURES BUILT ON FEEDBACK

Cultures of belief are data driven, not solely to measure or evaluate each individual in a pressurized performance quest, but to provide guidelines for improvement. These data-driven cultures serve to communicate to their members that every member of the team has value to the team.

Jack Clark, America's winningest rugby coach, maintains that as a coaching staff, they are "neurotic about capturing, sorting and publishing, at least internally. . . . We are always auditing our efforts to assess if we are on the right track. Where can we get better?" This constant drive of the coach to improve the performance of the team through careful and unbiased evaluation makes this cycle of effort and improvement a fixed part the culture.

For the last two years, I have had the opportunity to witness the Springfield volleyball culture build on the effort and preparation of the coach, which has become contagious and a driving force in the lives of the players. Every day, after every practice, players are emailed an elaborate statistical analysis of their performance that day in practice. The message is clear to starters and non-starters. Every job is on the line, *every day*. This feedback also creates a roadmap for players on how to improve.

Players, before a game at Springfield, receive detailed reports on every player, set, and tendency of the opponent that they will face that week. This level of effort not only prepares the team for every situation that they will face, but it creates a belief that there is no way that the opponent can win.

TRANSFORMATIONAL LEADERSHIP

What strikes you about belief in successful programs, beyond respect of the players for the coach, is the respect of the coach for the players. Players on these teams sense that the involvement with this coach is a life-changing experience beyond winning and losing games. Coaches build this effort in players by creating a climate of respect that is a two-way street. The culture of effort and belief extends far beyond the season or career of the athlete.

When one of his volleyball players from Puerto Rico struggled with language issues in the classroom, Coach Sullivan mirrored his week, attending classes with the player to discover what second-language issues may have been most challenging for the player. At times during the season, to build the comfort level of the players from Puerto Rico, and at the same time create sensitivity in his own players, Coach Sullivan will have a grad student from Puerto Rico run the practice only speaking Spanish, so that his players who speak English will experience performing in practice when listening to a coach who does not speak their native tongue, and therefore experience what the players from Puerto Rico experience every day.

Players know, based on experiences that go beyond the field or court, the coach's feeling for them is *beyond winning*. This belief that they are more than cogs in a winning team inspires more effort than cultures that are built solely around winning. Effort and belief combine to create a culture that is

SHOT CHARTS

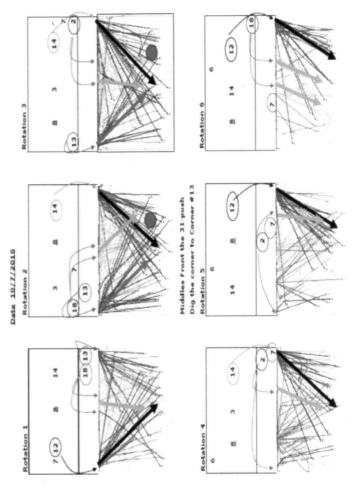

Figure 7.1. Springfield Pregame Data on Shot Charts. Author created.

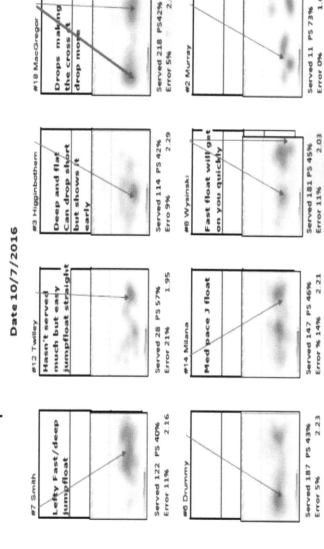

Figure 7.2.   Pregame Data on Heat Maps. Author created.

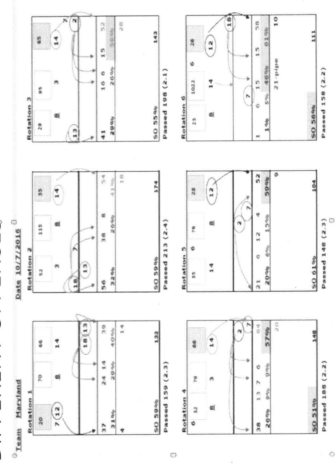

Figure 7.3. Springfield Pregame Data on Different Offenses. Author created.

SHOT CHARTS

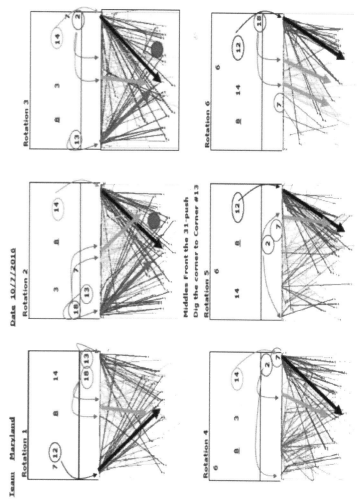

Figure 7.4. Springfield Pregame Data on Shot Charts. Author created.

unbeatable in any field. Without a culture built on mutual belief and effort, there is little chance that any organization can progress.

Five Takeaways from *Belief*

1. The belief that drives success begins with the unceasing work ethic of the leader.
2. Coaches on teams that win all the time have uncovered insights into the game through sustained effort and life experience that players believe will result in victory, and will at the same time actualize the player.
3. Effort is a two-way street, as players are driven through conformity to exhibit an effort that matches the intensity of the leader. If they do not match this effort, they are soon gone, regardless of ability.
4. There is a belief in the players that the coaches concern for them as people extends beyond the winning and losing of games.
5. Cultures of belief are built on data-driven cultures that make each player accountable for every practice and game. This use of data becomes the pathway for continuous improvement.

The Big Idea from *Belief*

Cultures of belief are built on the work ethic of the coach, which results in a mutual work ethic by player. These cultures are transformative for their members, who are actualized as players and as people as a result of being part of the culture.

8

Process

The more concerned we become over things we can't control, the less we will do with the things that we can control.

—John Wooden, UCLA Basketball

You cannot worry about end results. It's what you control every minute of the day.

—Nick Saban, Alabama Football

Process creates the roots of our program. The results are the fruits. We need to water the roots, enjoy the fruits, and quickly refocus on taking care of the roots some more.

—Charles Sullivan, Springfield Volleyball

MAINTAINING FOCUS ON PROCESS OVER PRODUCT

Over three hundred students were turned away from a sold-out Blake Arena on the afternoon of the NCAA Volleyball Championship in the spring of 2017. Despite the sold-out arena, flowered with adoring fans and white towels, in the first set, everything that could go wrong for the Springfield volleyball *did*.

The cheering crowd was greeted by hyped-up Springfield serves that crashed violently into the net or were hit so hard that they caromed out of bounds by five feet. Kills or spikes, meant to deflate the opponent, were hit with such force that they landed two feet beyond the sideline. Springfield put forth a great deal of effort, in fact, maybe too much effort. New Paltz easily won this first set. Losing the first set is often the kiss of a death in any high-stakes volleyball match.

After their triumph in the first set, visiting New Paltz players were out of their minds with optimism and enthusiasm at having dominated Springfield so convincingly. You could feel that New Paltz now had the confidence that they could win the national championship. If you watched the Springfield team retreat to their sideline after the first set, you saw players take their seats on the bench with the disappointment and strain of pressure etched into their faces.

But, if you watched the sideline just a little bit longer, you watched the Springfield players' smile, then chuckle, and finally laugh out loud. As the players returned to the court for the second set, you had the sense that this was a brand-new game. Springfield went on to win that second set and then dominate the third and fourth sets to win their tenth championship in thirteen years.

What technical adjustments did Coach Sullivan make and, more importantly, what was the laughing about? If you were a spectator, as I was, this question would be running through your mind after the game. Why laugh after you lost the first set of the biggest match of the year?

This is what took place. Coach Sullivan, in a rare expression of extreme emotion, said to his team, "You've waited your whole life to play in this game, this arena, this venue, with this crowd for this championship and I can't believe it. You're blowing it."

Except, that was not exactly what he said. What he actually said was, "you're *fudging* blowing this." As a coach who rarely uses profanity, some of the players furtively looked at each other and then secretly smiled to each other as they knew what the coach had meant.

Noticing their smiles, Coach Sullivan challenged the players. "Are you smiling because I used the f word?" Although Coach Sullivan is demanding in practice, profanity is not a regular part of that intensity. "If that is the reason that you are smiling, if that is what made you smile, then I can use it again. In fact, I can say *fudge* as much as you want if it is going to get you to play Springfield volleyball."

Coach Sullivan had broken the tension and the cloud of the consequences of losing faded from their minds. This focus was replaced by laughter at the coach's use of the "f" word as opposed to their understanding of the "f" word. The laughter that emerged from the timeout was evident to everyone, including New Paltz players. When the huddle broke, Coach Sullivan clapped and sent his players back on the court. "Now let's go out there and play Springfield volleyball." That is exactly what they did.

There were no technical adjustments in that time out. The team had struggled because it had shifted its focus to the product, winning the game, and lost sight of the processes that had brought them to this level. Winning coaches are able to maintain a team's focus on process and fundamentals, whatever the score. Successful leaders, in all fields, maintain the focus of the group on the process and not the end goal.

THE POWER OF BEING IN THE MOMENT

What had happened to the Springfield players in that first set is all too common, not only to athletic teams, but to all of us in life. When we become fixated on the end result, our desired goal, we lose our attention on the process that will get us to that goal. Springfield volleyball players wanted that championship so badly they let emotion take over and lost their focus on process.

As Springfield fell behind in this first set, they tried to hit the ball just a little harder and fell behind even more on the scoreboard. In their preoccupation with the score, they had abandoned the serving process that got them to that final game. This happens to teams at all levels of competition and it afflicts individuals and organizations in all pursuits and fields. Focusing so intensely on the goal can result in losing sight of the process that got us to where we are.

The end goal is intoxicating and hypnotic. As illogical as this might sound, Coach Sullivan maintains the surest way *not* to win is to focus only on winning. Having your players chant, *win, win, win* before a big game might be the very thing that derails their focus on the processes needed to win. When focus shifts to the product over process, winning coaches refocus and bring their teams back to the processes that drive their success.

This same focus on results can afflict business. Apple computers maintain a superior place in the market for computers by steadfastly focusing on its core value of *thinking differently* to create products that improve life. The sales are the by-product of that goal, and not the goal itself. The company must continually reset and remind itself of that value and redefine itself to place on top on the market.

The origins of maintaining focus in sports on what needs to be done in the moment and not what has just happened or will happen were expressed in the classic work on attention, *The Inner Game of Tennis*, by Timothy Gallwey. Gallwey's work has become a foundational lynchpin in the thinking of Pete Carroll and of new coaching legend Steve Kerr.

Using the Gallwey book as a teaching tool, Kerr trains his players to focus only on the current moment and what needs to be done rather than overthinking past or future events. To practice this skill, Kerr will have ten-minute sessions of practice without talking. Players are driven only by their instinctive brain reactions to play on the court.

If players lose focus and become fixated on the past or future, they are provided with the idea of a reset button that will wipe out this devastating focus on what they cannot control. To hear firsthand the secrets of being in the moment, activate the link below to connect to the work that shaped the thinking of both Pete Carroll and Steve Kerr.

Figure 8.1. The Little Known Book That Shaped the Minds of Steve Carroll and Pete Carroll (https://www.si.com/nba/2016/05/26/steve -kerr-pete-carroll-nba-playoffs-inner-game-tennis-book).

WINNING BY NOT FOCUSING ON WINNING

In the culture of those coaches who win all the time, there is an unceasing attention to fundamentals. This focus comes to life through a deliberate focus on the execution of process over product. From Wooden to Belichick to Saban to Sullivan, coaches who win all the time demand their teams single-mindedly perfect the processes that lead to success. Ironically, as Coach Sullivan proposes, when a coach's only goal is winning the desired winning rarely happens.

In *Thinking Body, Dancing Mind*, Chungliang Al Huang and Jerry Lynch offer the reader a combination of Eastern philosophy and Western sport. The authors urge us to "let go of the obsessive desire to produce . . . and focus on the joy, the dance, the flow." This approach to being in the moment is keyed by the belief that our bodies know what to do instinctively when we are properly trained.

Overthinking about what we have to do has been the downfall of many athletes in pressure situations across every sport. Malcolm Gladwell describes the dangers of overthinking in pressure situations as "choking."

> When people get anxious about performing, they naturally become particularly self-conscious; they begin scrutinizing actions that are best performed on autopilot. The expert golfer, for instance, begins contemplating the details of his swing, making sure that the elbows are tucked and his weight is properly shifted. This kind of deliberation can be lethal for a performer.

Athletes from Michael Jordan to Billie Jean King have been driven by an approach built on performing in the moment, eliminating all other distraction. Billie Jean King proposes that the real joy of athletics is not the result, but the process. In her research, sports psychologist, Amy Baltzell of Boston

University, has deliberately applied these mindfulness principles to athletes to improve their peak performances.

Baltzell's book, *Living in the Sweet Spot: Preparing for Performance in Sport and Life*, shares specific strategies for helping athletes cope with minds that lose focus on process and become paralyzed by the fear involved in performance. Fear of failure is natural, and at times, these fears creep into our subconscious. Baltzell urges athletes to recognize and acknowledge these fears of failure and reset the mind to focus on process, rather than trying to ignore the feeling and the pressure of the moment.

Process-over-product focus is a key not only to success in sports but in all venues in life. Those seeking profit as the end game rarely attain long-term success. Simon Sinek provided the foundation for this process-over-product approach in his extraordinary TED video, "How Great Leaders Inspire Action." If leaders can shift the focus from the end result, the product to larger purposes defined by the organization's core values, they can become an organization that wins without focusing on winning.

Figure 8.2.   Start with the Why. (https://www.ted.com/talks/simon _sinek_how_great_leaders_inspire_action).

FOCUS ON PRODUCT BEGINS EARLY: A BASEBALL STORY

One of the major disadvantages of coaching on the collegiate level is that it is a struggle to find the time to be present at your own children's athletic contests. Shortly after his volleyball season ended, Coach Sullivan had the privilege of attending his son's little league baseball game. Ironically, the process-over-product concerns of this chapter are present even in youth competition. The dangers of a product preoccupation came to life for Coach Sullivan on that day far from the Blake Arena volleyball court.

Although not possessing the time to assume the role of assistant coach, Coach Sullivan has been awarded the status of unofficial assistant coach and serves as a mentor to his son's team when time allows. As a result of this role with the team, Coach Sullivan was seated next to the official coach in the dugout at his son's team's high-pressure playoff game.

This game was going along extremely well. The head coach's son, a natural athlete and a gifted baseball player, was pitching with power and poise. With a three-run lead, the young pitcher seemed unhittable, and the team seemed unbeatable. All of this changed in the final inning.

The gifted young pitcher suddenly could not throw a strike, and the more he pressed, the harder he threw, the more elusive the plate came for him. As this point, there was a clamor in the stands. Despite the league rules about inappropriate parental involvement as spectators, there were shouts and suggestions that it was time for a new pitcher. Even the coach's wife came to the dugout to ask her frustrated husband what he intended to do.

After several unsuccessful forays for mound conferences, the manager turned to Coach Sullivan. With the bases loaded, and the team nursing a one-run lead, Coach Sullivan walked to the mound. It was easy to see the frustration on the face of the young pitcher who was now on the verge of tears. Coach Sullivan's first words were that it was a hot day and it would be a great day for ice cream. He then asked the frustrated young man if he liked ice cream.

The mound conference then turned to a discussion on ice cream. When Coach Sullivan asked the young man what his favorite flavor of ice cream, the young man responded, vanilla. The coach looked shocked at such a response. "Vanilla?, what about Rocky Road, Cherry Garcia, and more exotic ice creams?" The coach confessed that when he takes a spoonful of one of these unusual ice cream flavors, the next thing he knows, the pint is gone.

Finally, Coach Sullivan looked at the young man and concluded, "Listen, why don't you just throw a strike and we will go get some ice cream." The boy smiled and the next pitch was a blazing fastball and a called strike three. The game was over. When the astonished coach approached Coach Sullivan at game's end, he asked what was said. Coach Sullivan jokingly responded, "I'm a professional coach. I can't give those secrets away."

The secret was that by focusing on the product, a strike or the win, the young man had abandoned his fundamentals. John Wooden's players report, to a man, that despite winning more national collegiate basketball championships than any other coach in the sport's history, Wooden never in their four years with him ever mentioned the idea or necessity of winning. Wooden's focus was entirely on process, and shifting that focus to the results or products can derail any of us from little leaguer to professional.

Five Takeaways from *Process*

1. The focus on product can derail any individual who may abandon fundamentals in a concern about the result or outcome of the contest.
2. Great athletes possess mindfulness, focusing on the moment, not dwelling on the past or the future.
3. The surest way not to win is to focus only on winning.

4. Mindfulness does not arise on its own, but it is a direct result of a coach's planning and emphasis on this state of being as part of the culture's core values.
5. In business, focusing on profits rather than the process of creating a perfect product is exactly the same as a sports team focusing on winning without giving attention to the fundamentals needed to ensure that winning.

The Big Idea from *Process*

The focus for winning teams is always on process, seeking to perfect that process rather than the short-term results of and products of that process.

9

Identity

A person doesn't really become whole until he becomes part of something bigger than himself.

—Jim Valvano, North Carolina State

Individual commitment to a group effort—that's what makes a team work, a company work, a society work, a civilization work.

—Vince Lombardi

When people do things that they weren't even sure they were capable of, I think it comes back to connection. Connection with teammates. Connection with organization. Connection with the environment. I think it's a human need to feel connected.

—Theo Epstein, Chicago Cubs

WHICH RING?

It was NCAA time again and Springfield's lacrosse team was again ready for Coach Sullivan's NCAA pregame speech. This lacrosse team was much stronger than the unsure team that introduced this book. This team had high hopes of going deeper in the tournament than previous teams that Coach Sullivan had addressed. In fact, this team had hopes of winning it all.

The message presented in that talk was one that will resonate with the players for their entire lives and an example of the power of identity that the reader might consider sharing with their teams and organizations. The story that Coach Sullivan shared with the lacrosse team captures the essence of identity that is the culminating ingredient in the cultural grit recipe.

Coach Sullivan began this speech from a totally different vantage point than his visit in our earlier chapter. "I hear you guys are pretty good and you have the potential to reach the final rounds of this year's NCAA tournament. Around campus, the word is, you have the talent to win the whole thing if you play well." The team smiled, enjoying the praise that they had the ability to be champions. The team was taken aback by Coach Sullivan's next challenge.

"I'll tell you what. I have nine of our NCAA championship rings from previous volleyball teams at Springfield. Since I know you might be earning one soon, why don't you pick one out for your championship. If you pick the right one, I can guarantee you, you will soon be wearing your own ring." Although this was a rather outrageous claim, the team had a strong belief that the words of Coach Sullivan were forged on insights beyond their comprehension.

The team now meticulously went through enlarged pictures of the nine rings and came to consensus on the one ring that they would select should they win. As the team presented their choice to Charlie, he slowly shook his head. "You picked the wrong ring." The team sat dumbfounded and deflated by this simple pronouncement. The team was confused that there could be a right answer to such a question.

"The ring you picked is likely to be the reason that you won't win it all. The ring you picked is about bragging, about telling the world what you did. If you wanted to win, you should have picked this ring." With this, Coach Sullivan then held up his left hand, revealing his wedding ring.

"This is a ring that signifies a commitment to another person, a vow that you will be there for them, no matter what, forever." What followed was an explanation that to win a championship, you have to place the needs of the team in front of your own needs and goals. Your commitment has to be to something greater than yourself. Your identity as a team member has to replace your individual goals.

This wedding ring story is the peak of the pyramid for championship teams. On these teams, the needs of the individual are truly secondary to the needs of the team. When teams reach their potential, they become *we*. After winning three national championships in a row, the Springfield volleyball players were asked, *"Why were we so successful?"* All, but one player, answered the same, "team cohesion."

THE POWER OF IDENTITY

The power of culture is that conformity drives our performance up a notch to meet the standard of the group, but truly exceptional teams and organizations affect more than behavior, they affect our identity. The norms and values of a team, become who we are and supersede our individual needs. In our goal pursuits, this identity causes us to forsake personal costs and benefits as our motivator and to become driven more by team goal pursuits. Our identity as a team member becomes the driver of our decisions.

Angela Duckworth suggests that when cultures are really successful, members often use a noun that describes the organization to identify who they are. *I am a Packer*, *a Patriot*, and in the case of Angela Duckworth's father, who worked for the DuPont Motor Company, *a Duponter*. This power to identify as a member of a culture is the apex of the grit pyramid.

The father of positive psychology, Martin Seligman, asserts that we truly flourish when we move beyond the hedonic needs of self to find purpose or meaning in something greater than self-benefit. This identity transformation may be the "secret sauce" that truly great teams possess in the face of setbacks and obstacles that would discourage others.

In all of the great teams, you will see players rise above the expectations of others. There are a good number of factors at play. Of course, there is the power of conformity and increased effort to meet a higher standard of the team. The power of identity drives a purpose greater than self, but there is something else at play in dynastic teams. There is a social multiplier effect responsible for superior teams.

The social multiplier effect is that the players on these teams actually make one another greater though the culture. On every team that wins multiple championships, you will find gritty and talented players that compete at truly extraordinary levels. After championships, these players in post-game interviews will consistently pay homage to their teammates. As we watch these interviews, we cannot help but be struck by not only the love that the team has for one another, but also the humility of the exceptional players.

Psychologist Jim Flynn proposes that "the great player becomes greater and grittier because the grit of one player influences the grit of another in profound ways." Think of a team made up of this type of player and you will understand the transformational power of a team to create grit in its members. As stated earlier, this idea that great teams make great players is counterintuitive to our notions of sport and how sports in America are defined.

Our basic belief is that the easiest way to win a championship is to assemble great players, and this will translate to a great team. The idea that the team is what makes the player great might at first glance seem backwards. However, the current Warriors team (2018), a team made up of superstar players, has had to become great team in order to achieve their goals. Sports is riddled with unsuccessful teams of superstar players who never forged that team identity.

DEBUNKING THE GREAT PLAYER MYTH

Some will challenge this notion that identity as a team member may be more important than the talent of the players who make up the team. Turn on sports talk radio and the banter is constant, measuring the talent and concluding that the reason that teams win all of the time is all too obvious. Teams that win all the time are simply made up of the best players.

Opponents insist Springfield volleyball wins simply because they have these best players, year in and year out. Undoubtedly, Springfield and teams that win all the time are made up of truly outstanding athletes and great players. Does greatness in players create these great teams or does the greatness in the team produce the greatness in the players?

Springfield volleyball seeks to find the most talented players that it can, as do all competitive teams. Players that make up the Springfield roster come with pedigrees and are recruited from as far away as Puerto Rico and California. Springfield recruits these players without the ability to give athletic scholarships. Legendary players have defined the Springfield tradition, but which came first, the chicken or the egg? Did participation and identity in the culture give rise to the greatness or did the greatness of the player create the culture?

Every year, extraordinary, nationally recognized players graduate from Springfield College, and after each of those graduations, Springfield's opponents exhale a sigh of relief, believing that with the exodus of these great players Springfield will now be beatable again. However, the next run of players, with unrecognizable names fills in with little or no difference in the performance of the team. Talented players make up the roster of the Springfield team, but these great players rise to the next level, to a great extent, as products of the culture.

If you examine any sport dynasty, you will come to the realization that it is more than great players behind the winning. It is something else. A critic of UCLA's ten-championship run claimed that UCLA won because Coach Wooden had the *horses*. By *horses*, the critic meant that UCLA only won because they had the best players in the nation. John Wooden's response to that critic holds for Springfield, and all dynastic teams.

Wooden is reported to have said, "It is true that we have great players, or the horses as you like to say about us, and we have players of this caliber, year after year. But there are many teams, who do have the horses, and do not win."

The secret of dynasties is that extraordinary players come to Springfield volleyball, and they came to UCLA basketball, *because of the culture*. Players instinctively sense that these cultures will make them into the best players that they can be. Great players are drawn to great cultures that are about more than winning and losing.

Teams that win year after year do so with great players, not just because of those great players, but because of a culture forged on effort and belief. In these teams, the identity of the team comes to override personal desires, and it is transformative for the players. Players instinctively know that certain cultures will help them actualize as the best version of themselves on the playing field and *in life.*

TEAM IDENTITY BUILT ON GREAT COMMUNICATION

Some feel that team identity should flow naturally as an outcome of being on a great team. However, if you study teams that win all the time, you will uncover the effort that coaches of these teams devote to communicating and living the team identity. Team identity is not built in the opening meeting, but is reinforced by relentless communication and reinforcing of the message. Great coaches are great communicators.

Duckworth captures what great coaches do in her analysis of Pete Carroll in a visit to the Seahawk's training camp. Duckworth shares Carroll insights on how he creates a team identity:

> He [Carroll] tells me it's not just one thing. It's a million things. It's a million details. It's substance and it's style. After a day with the Seahawks, I have to agree. It is countless small things . . . so easy to botch, forget, or ignore. And though the details are countless, there are some themes. The most obvious is language. . . . *You are a Seahawk 24–7.*

What emerges from these practices is that team identity grows from the leader living out and communicating the team's values in daily practices.

If you were to visit a Springfield volleyball practice, you might find Coach Sullivan carrying a rolled-up copy of the Springfield Core Values. When players do not execute to the expectations of the values, Coach Sullivan will sit with the player and point to a specific technique to have a player refocus their efforts. After one disappointing first-half performance, Coach Sullivan actually read the core values to the team. Instead of placing a half-time adjustment, the restating and reaffirmation of values resulted in a reinvigorated second-half performance.

What emerges is the power of language and culture in communicating team values. This is true not only for Carroll and the Seahawks, but for every coach who wins all the time. It is not just what you say and how often you say it, but how you get your message across. Anson Dorrance, North Carolina's legendary women's soccer coach, has his team memorize quotes that encapsulate the team's core values.

Charlie Sullivan has his team do a common read and builds the read into daily practice sessions. After reading Duckworth's *Grit: The Power of Passion and Perseverance*, players ended practices focusing on what they liked about each other's passion in the practice. Winning coaches paint a picture with their vocabulary and live that vocabulary every day of their lives. The by-product of that team identity is that although players are competing for position, they come to love one another and are bonded in ways that defy the nature of their daily competition for starting spots. Below, the Seahawks talk about the evolution of their culture and language, epitomized by the phrase *LOB, love our brother*.

Figure 9.1. How Pete Carroll created a winning culture in Seattle (https://www.youtube.com/watch?v=DMaIpCxtSfM). Author created.

The takeaway is that great leaders spend the time to create a culture driven by an identity shaped by their core values. It is not enough to merely post these values on a bulletin board, for core values will be tested daily. Jack Clark, of Cal Berkeley rugby, the winningest coach in the history of rugby, relates stories of players coming into the coaching room and fumbling in their effort to discuss playing time.

This is in direct contradiction to the team value of *team first, self last*. Clark relates, "Finally they just say, 'You're going to ask me what's best for the team, aren't you?' And I say, of course I am going to ask you that. The value of selflessness, forsaking personal gain for team needs 'in making decisions solves ten problems.'" It is not just a common vocabulary or enthusiastic organization that creates team identity, but living the values that drive your organization on a daily basis.

COLLECTIVE EFFICACY: THE RESEARCH BEHIND TEAM COHESION

The success of the coaches and programs cited in this work is not without scientific explanation in the research on human development. Albert Bandura, back in the 1970s, identified a key factor in the success of groups as the "group's shared belief in its conjoint capability to organize and execute the courses of action responsible for success." Bandura's observation was that a group's greater belief in its abilities as a group was consistently associated with greater success.

Bandura named this phenomenon *collective efficacy*, and a plethora of research in a host of domains has documented the effectiveness of *collective efficacy* in predicting success. John Hattie, in *Visible Learning*, a meta-analysis of the research on what is most effective in producing school success, reports effect sizes in which collective efficacy has been demonstrated to be more than double any other factor in resulting in the success of a school.

Hattie suggests that we reset the narrative for schools, as "collective efficacy does not happen serendipitously or by accident. School leaders must work to build a culture designed to increase collective efficacy." Careful study of the Springfield volleyball program has demonstrated to me that this mission of building culture is a continuous one and a never-ending struggle to maintain collective efficacy in a self-centered world.

To follow Charles Sullivan through a season is to experience an unceasing struggle to maintain collective efficacy in handling the challenges players face. At the outset of the season, players are challenged to replace the term *expectation* with the term *excitement*. Maintaining the team's *excitement* and their collective efficacy is a constant challenge as the season develops, and individual desires for success arise to threaten those goals.

FOSTERING COLLECTIVE EFFICACY AT SPRINGFIELD

Coach Sullivan estimates that he spends twice as much time in creating techniques to foster and build team cohesion than he does in working on strategy and training. His creativity in building a cohesive unit is unparalleled.

One of the issues that had the potential to ruin the Springfield volleyball team was the historic conflicts that existed between the geographic regions of the players who make up the team. The team has been largely made of players from the hotbeds of volleyball, Puerto Rico and California. Conflict results from the fact that these two areas are major rivals in the world of volleyball and there is often no love lost for each other by players from each area.

To deal with the issue head on, Coach Sullivan came to one practice with several plain brown paper bags. Selecting one of the players from Puerto Rico, Coach Sullivan asked the player to reach into the bag, take a handful of the contents and eat what he had fished out. With disgust, the player spit out the plain flour that he had just tasted.

Taking a different bag, a player from California was asked to do the same. That player also wincingly spit out the plain grain seeds from the bag that he had just taken in. At this point, selecting another player, Coach Sullivan produced a slice of whole grain bread, slathered in butter, from a third bag.

As this player contentedly chewed on the bread, Coach Sullivan explained that the team had a choice. They could remain as Puerto Ricans and Californians, playing their separate brand of volleyball as rivals, and the result would be as distasteful as the bags of flour and grain. The other option is that they could come together as a team and make delicious bread. Which was it going to be?

On a different visit to practice later in the season, after the team read of *The Ideal Team Player*, by Patrick Lencioni. Coach then produced a set of charts in which players had rated each other on the traits that Lencioni had researched as resulting in optimum business performance and increased *collective efficacy*. Those terms, *hungry*, *humble*, and *smart*, became the formula for players working on their traits as teammates, building team cohesion and not their skills as volleyball players.

The terms, *hungry*, *humble*, and *smart* refer to characteristics that players rated themselves on, but Sullivan translated these terms into the virtues of *humility*, *working hard*, *and people-smarts*, *relationships*. To make the definitions understandable and meaningful for his team, the chart below defines those characteristics as translated to volleyball.

Each coach rated each player and the players rated themselves. In a step later in the season, each player rated his teammates. What emerged was that some of the best players had a good deal of work to do as teammates. Each player was given not only a score, but also the list of character-driven actions that they needed to work on as the season progressed.

The amount of volleyball that goes into preparation in getting this team ready for an NCAA championship is staggering, but the amount of effort in building collective efficacy is twice the volleyball effort. Practice on a given day might begin with clips from *The Matrix*, Mr. Miyagi and *The Karate Kid*, Will Smith, and more examples of motivators too numerous to cite. In fact, in working on the book, I was continually astonished to learn that the previous efforts at team building had been supplanted with newer ones, making the task of keeping up with Coach Sullivan nearly impossible.

On the final plane ride to the 2018 NCAA Championship game this year, Coach Sullivan, noting the rising anxiety as the game was rapidly approaching, left the team with these thoughts. "Nothing to do with our success is about any one of you as an individual. This is about our team, and if you begin to think it is about your performance alone, you will not be able to shoulder that burden and you will not help us." This thought defines Springfield volleyball.

TEXTBOX 9.1. VIRTUES DEFINITIONS:
Humility, Work Hard, People-Smarts Relationships

Humility

1. Others first is OK
2. Secure with yourself—not insecure
3. Don't need self-acclaim or attention
4. Helps others succeed
5. Confident in their skills—avoid acting humble because you are not confident and acting humble hides this insecurity—not genuine
6. Taking responsibilities for errors

Work Hard

1. Dives for balls that hit the floor
2. Extra effort—more than what is asked
3. Extra intensity level
4. Extra effort toward footwork and communicating
5. Doing extra things without being asked—taking nets up and down, meeting
6. Expectations in the dorms
7. Volunteering for responsibilities
8. Working on the team outside the court

People-Smarts, Relationships

1. Dealing with people
2. Listening and communicating effectively—building relationships
3. Investing in relationships with your teammates
4. Taking time to build relationships with teammates to build trust
5. Avoiding isolation
6. Treat other people well—they feel good as a result of you

Once these virtues are performed well, we can invest our time in digesting our Core Values.

On the first day of practice, long before that plane ride, Springfield players were handed a printed packet defining the team's core principles. Key among those values is the word *represent*. This word means that Springfield players represent something greater than their own accomplishments. In fact, on and off the court, Springfield players represent something beyond winning. This sense of purpose is what brings about championships and gives rise to a level of cultural grit that is hard for opponents to match.

Five Takeaways from *Identity*

1. As counterintuitive as it may seem, great cultures make great players and not the reverse.
2. Assembling great players on one team will not guarantee success. Outsiders viewing winning teams tend to reduce the success of those teams to the great players on those teams. Insiders know it is far more than great players. It is a culture built on shared belief.
3. Great players seek out great teams, recognizing that these teams have a culture that will bring out their greatness. Great players are drawn to great cultures.
4. Collective efficacy, the belief in the effectiveness of your group, is the researched explanation for group success in all endeavors. Building collective efficacy is not a one-time effort, but a continuing quest to find ways to instill it in your team.
5. In great cultures, players are willing to replace personal goals with team goals. The identity of the player is now defined by being a member of the organization rather than personal identity.

The Big Idea from *Identity*

When organizations are truly successful in creating a culture of belief, participants in that culture enjoy a relationship with the organization that creates their purpose and identity in life and a motivation that moves team goals in front of personal goals.

MAINTAINING BELIEF

Cultures under Fire

Well, if you really want a guy and you don't get him, that's OK. He'll only beat you once a year. On the other hand, if you get the wrong guy on your team, he'll beat you every day.

—Bo Schembechler

Good teams become great ones when the team members trust each other to surrender the me for the we.

—Phil Jackson

Leadership is the potent combination of strategy and character. But if you must be without one, be without strategy.

—Norman Schwarzkopf

THE HAIRCUT: HOLDING FAST TO CORE VALUES IN THE FACE OF CHALLENGE

Bill Walton, returning NCAA player of the year on UCLA's national basketball championship team, became swept up in the counterculture protest movement of the sixties and approached legendary coach John Wooden before the team's first practice. Walton had decided to challenge the coach's hair-length rule, embracing his convictions and the spirit of the times. At issue was Coach Wooden's firm team rule that hair length could not exceed two inches and facial hair was strictly prohibited.

Walton opened his challenge to Wooden's right to dictate the hair length of his players from a legal, constitutional standpoint, claiming that a coach did not have the legal right to dictate hair length. Walton believed that this was a violation of the players' rights guaranteed under the United States Constitution. Walton further argued that his extensive research could not find any links between hair length and basketball play.

Wooden responded, "I admire people who stand up for their beliefs. You're right, Bill, I do not have the right to say how long people can wear their hair. I do have the right to say who can play on this team. We are going to miss you." The result, grown larger in the retelling, was that Walton borrowed and furiously rode a bicycle to the campus barber, returning with his hair cut to the proper length before practice.

What is revealed in this story is a deep insight into why some coaches win all the time. Coaches who win all the time have a code of core values and a set of principles that are developed after deep and reflective experience. They live by that core and defend that core in the face of challenge. Codes of conduct are like opinions; every coach has one. Coaches who win all the time maintain that code when those values are under siege.

More than a guide for a team or suggested practices, the core values of truly winning cultures are lived on a daily basis and define every decision of the team. There are not many coaches in America who would have been willing to follow a set of core values that might have sacrificed the best player in the nation over hair length. What was at issue in the controversy was not hair length; it was preserving the core values of the team.

The truth is that this was an issue that would determine whether the values that defined the team were greater than the whim and will of an individual who came into conflict with those values. The fact that the challenge came from the most talented player in the nation made that challenge more dramatic and memorable.

Most coaches might have agonized over the potential loss of America's premiere player, but Wooden never blinked or wavered. Truly extraordinary coaches live the words of Robert Kennedy, that you stand up for what you believe in, or you fall down for everything. Maintaining core values affirms that the needs and desires of the individual are secondary to the needs of the team.

Although Walton was going through a period of his life where he challenged authority, even the authority of the United States government to wage war in Vietnam, he knew instinctively that this challenge to his coach was one that he could not win. As free-spirited a guy as Walton was, he knew that the values and practices of the UCLA basketball team were greater than any single player.

Not only did Walton learn from this challenge to core values, but every player on that team learned the same lessons from Coach Wooden's stand. This same characteristic of maintaining belief in the face of threats to those beliefs is present in an analysis of any coach who wins all the time. The careers of America's legendary winning coaches are built on the foundation that the interests of an individual do not take precedence over the values that define the team.

How else can anyone explain Bill Belichick's trading of Randy Moss after Moss's banner year in receptions, never fully discussing the reasons but stressing the decision was about *the welfare of the team*. The reasons for the trade were never fully revealed, but how many coaches trade one of the NFL's reception leaders after a season in which the receiver leads the league?

In a classic YouTube presentation, Geno Auriemma brings to life this same respect for the modern-day maintenance of cores values. Sharing his feelings over how difficult it is to be a young basketball player today in an era of chest thumping, breast beating, and *me first* examples from the professional ranks, Geno goes on to share the core values that define his team. Although his style, delivery, and approach are different than Wooden's, the values are identical.

What is striking is that Auriemma looks beyond just the players' actions in a game. He has made it a practice to study the reactions of players, when they are out of the game. He studies their body language to discover how they feel about the teammates playing in mop-up sections of the game, promising that players who are not team-first oriented, supporting every member of the team, will never see the floor for a University of Connecticut basketball team.

Further, Auriemma relates sitting one of his best players in a key game, not for motivational reasons, but for failing to live up to the core values of team-first play. Listen in below to get a feel for the intensity of maintaining core values that define America's coaches.

Figure 10.1. Geno Auriemma on Body Language and Recruiting Enthusiastic Kids (https://www.youtube.com/watch?v=LYP7H-SumdQ). Author created.

Sidney Wicks was one the most talented basketball players in the nation in his time at UCLA. Sidney came to Wooden at the start of his junior year, wondering why he was not starting. Wooden responded that although Wicks may have been the second-most-talented player ever in his coaching at UCLA, it was a shame that he might never get to play there if he didn't learn to value the needs of team over self. Belief is built not on the words of the coach but on the actions of the coach in preserving those words. Talk is cheap.

When Sidney Wicks would urge John Wooden to put him into games early in his career, insisting to Wooden that he put him in because he was the best player, Wooden had a simple, but short response. *You may be the best player on the team, but the team does not play best when you are in.* When Sidney learned to value the needs of team over self, he did go on to be named the best player in the nation.

At Springfield, when beginning this book, I asked Coach Sullivan why he lost his first game of the season in California. He responded that it was most probably because he did not play his best player, a player who would later be voted the nation's best player. That player had failed to live up to the effort representative of the culture, and Coach Sullivan demonstrated to the team that the rules on his team applied to all of the members.

Coaches who share the belief that no player, no matter how great, is greater than the core values that define the team must be willing to act on that belief. Players must know and believe that the core values that define a program will last long after the opening meeting. On great teams, on first encounter, players understand their individual needs are secondary to the team's needs. They also learn that challenges to this premise will result in dismissal from the team.

TEAM FIRST: EVEN WHEN IT HURTS

Before the 2013 NCAA final, the statistical analysis of the opponent in that final NCAA volleyball championship game revealed that the team was better served by starting a player who had not started a game all season. Based on this player's unique skills and the capacities of the team that they faced in the final, it was clear that the team's lineup needed to be adjusted for the final game if the team was to capitalize on its strengths.

As clear-cut as the decision was on paper, in real life, decisions involve people that are not as clear-cut. This decision required telling a senior starter for a team that was ranked number one in offense for the entire season that the team would be stronger if he did not start the final game. Even more potentially insulting to the player was the fact that this switch also involved the once starting senior to come in as a designated server in the game.

This was a decision for the benefit of the team, but it didn't make it any less painful for both player and coach. After tears on the part of both, the player agreed that the only option was to support the decision that the coach believed to be in the best interest of the team. The team went on to win that national championship, and the senior replaced in the final game came in to serve his team to the championship, scoring on a remarkable 85 percent of his service attempts with over five aces.

This decision certainly contributed to the success of the team on this day, but even more importantly, the power of this decision reinforced the team's core values. The welfare of the team was always first, and all decisions are centered on what is in the best interests of the team, even those decisions that have the potential to hurt an individual. This story, legend now in the history of Springfield volleyball, established forever that the concept of team first was more than words.

MAINTAINING BELIEF: GETTING ON THE BUS WITH ELMO

Belief is easily maintained at the start of a season, but as the season wears on, the drain and strain take a toll mentally and physically. Volleyball, in effect, is at high intensity for most of the year. By April, most players tend to fade, but not at Springfield. April at Springfield is special. Coach Sullivan has made the month of April a personal challenge to every player who plays for Springfield. The month of April concludes with the national championship, the ultimate goal of every team at Springfield

If you go to most practices of the Springfield volleyball, you will experience the familiar routines that make up a culture and define preparation. There is energy, and you can feel that the routines are deeply embedded in every player. The players seem to go through these routines almost without the coaches. However, if you go on April 1, you will experience something entirely different from the routines you have come to know during the season.

You may find the gym decorated and flashing lights or games set up to challenge the team or you may be introduced to the power of Elmo. April 1 is a special day for every Springfield team that Charlie Sullivan coaches. It is the day that they are invited to get on the bus to the championship. The day clarifies the ultimate team goal and generally the effort and feelings in that championship quest stay with them for life. April 1 offers players the opportunity to be champions.

On this first day of April, Springfield players are asked to recommit to the core of values that drive the program. This celebration of the team recommitting to the goal of a championship is a tradition at Springfield. Players find the locker room plastered with emails from past programs, reminding players of the tradition and the opportunity in front of them as April begins (see appendix B).

This past year, at the end of the season, players were told in advance that a world-renowned psychologist would lecture the team on what they might need to capture this championship. The players, on entering the gym, were then greeted by the *Sesame Street* character, Elmo, singing the song, "Imagination" in a projected video on forty-foot screen.

After the laughter died down at the end of the song, players were challenged with the question of why Elmo was beginning their April practice in the stretch run to the NCAA tournament. A host of answers affirmed the idea that limits to performance, as Elmo sings, are only the limits of our own imagination. The real limit to our performance is our limiting thoughts and doubts. The air was tinged with excitement as the practice began.

"Can we hit .400 in baseball?" Coach Sullivan challenged the team on April 1. "Certainly, the number 400 is only a limitation in our mind." Coach Sullivan reminded the team that they had shattered previously thought-of limits in the hitting percentage by ignoring what was thought to be the limit. Finally, Coach Sullivan reminded the team that they control their thoughts, and their thoughts control their actions. There is no limit to their performance, if they can control their thoughts. In effect, they can accomplish what they can imagine.

The team took in this talk and ended the practice with the reenergized resolve that defines every team in Coach Sullivan's tenure. Though laughter was present at the start of practice, in the end, there was more focus than in any previous practice. It was then that Coach Sullivan announced that at this practice they were getting on the bus to the NCAA championship and welcomed all to get on the bus. "This is your opportunity. Will you be remembered or forgotten? Will you commit and get on the bus or not?" The players all got on the bus, as they do every year.

THE REAL CHALLENGE: MAINTAINING BELIEF IN BUILDING YOUR CULTURE

What goes unsaid in this narrative is that the struggle that one faces in creating a culture built on a foundation of cultural grit is a natural and necessary part of the process. In the sport of men's college lacrosse there is no more successful or iconic coach than Bill Tierney, currently of the University of Denver, but renowned for transforming Princeton University into one of the most successful programs in the history of American lacrosse.

What most students of lacrosse know about Coach Tierney is that his extraordinary winning percentage (.730) and success in NCAA championships most closely resembles that of Coach Sullivan in volleyball at Springfield College. Although Coach Tierney has won a record seven NCAA Division I tournaments, his winning six titles in nine years at Princeton University is a truly remarkable accomplishment, given the fact that Princeton has more of a reputation for scholarship than for athletics and is prohibited from offering athletic aid.

When Coach Tierney is mentioned in coaching circles, the only image that comes to mind is that of his success in final games. On every level of lacrosse, Coach Tierney's record is synonymous with success and championships, but few know that the foundation of this success is built on struggle, adversity, and maintaining belief at the beginning of his program in the face of hardships.

As with all successful coaches, the road to championships was paved with little-talked-about challenges to their core of beliefs. The real struggle for all coaches or leaders is to maintain belief and hold fast to those core values in the face of failure. Revitalizing or building a culture is a necessary pathway that Bill Walsh of the San Francisco Forty Niners, Bill Belichick of the Patriots, and even John Wooden of the UCLA Bruins endured.

When we picture winning coaches, we do not often recall the painful steps needed to build their championship programs. Ending this story with a personal recounting of the first season of Coach Tierney might offer hope to beginning culture creators in the face of the challenge that the early years bring.

In 1988, Coach Tierney's first team at Princeton University went 2–13 and 0–6 in the Ivy League. This has personal connections for me, because, the twelfth loss, a 12–6 setback in that initial season took place at Adelphi University. I was part of the coaching staff of that Adelphi team and my concern at the end of that game was not for Princeton, but for the well-being of Coach Tierney.

What concerned me as a friend of Bill's was that in his struggle to transform the culture, he seemed to be affected, beyond wins and losses. Bill had lost a good deal of weight, appeared to be aging prematurely, and was physically exhausted. I know, because I asked him to take a walk with me after the game out of my concerns over his well-being. I was not sure that he would survive the move from America's most storied program, Johns Hopkins, to the challenge of transforming this needy Princeton program.

What will always stay with me was the commitment in Coach Tierney's voice and his eyes. He was respectful and allayed my concerns for his well-being, but assured me that he was going to turn this all around at Princeton. The strength of his commitment came through in our brief walk and talk. At that moment, I knew his resolve and belief could move mountains and that it would not be wise to bet against Princeton in the near future. Despite this ominous beginning, Coach Tierney maintained belief.

To create and maintain belief is a constant challenge for coaches and leaders. Nowhere is that challenge greater for beginning coaches than in building the foundation of that culture. This process will test your resolve, and maintaining belief in the face of failure will be the greatest challenge that you face. This challenge will also provide you with the greatest rewards in your life.

Five Takeaways from *Cultures under Fire*

1. Players on teams that maintain core values know after the first meeting with the team that the needs of the team will outweigh their individual wants and desires.
2. Players who fail to honor the team's core values cannot be a part of the team, no matter how talented.
3. Effort and belief can fade as a season wears on, and a coach must address the need for staying power.
4. Maintaining effort and belief when changing or creating a culture is a true test of a coach's commitment and resolve. What goes unsaid in this book is that the coaches who win all the time have all endured the test of maintaining belief in the face of early challenge.
5. There needs to be a tangible challenge to team members to commit to the end goal, and this commitment must be all consuming. This commitment to excellence, which comes when motivation may be slipping, rekindles passion and effort and has impacts that shape the rest of the players' lives.

The Big Idea from *Cultures under Fire*

For organizations to be truly successful, leaders must not only create and communicate core values, but they must also maintain those values when they are challenged. Those values must become the deciding instrument in every decision that the organization makes and in every direction that the organization undertakes.

Postscript from Coach Sullivan

Raise Your Hand: Applications to Business

This is a fun little activity I do to start my business presentations. I tell the crowd that I want to get an idea of what type of group I am working with today so I am going to give them a little test. I inform the group that when I say *go*, I want them to raise their hand as high as possible and then wait for further instructions.

For effect, I throw in a line about how I really need a good concentrated effort from the group to get the most from this activity. Then I say *go*, and everyone raises their hand high. Occasionally, someone will stand on their chair to get their hand higher. "Love that intensity," I say when that happens.

After a quick few seconds, when everyone has his or her hand in the air, I say, "OK, now raise your hand a little higher." The group invariably raises their hands a few inches higher. After some chuckles and laughs, I say, "How did that happen? I am going to give this group the benefit of the doubt and not assume from this activity that you are all poor listeners."

We review how everyone raised their hand as high as they could and when I said a little higher, everyone had a little more to give. I call this difference "The Achievement Gap." That is difference between good teams and championship teams. Everyone has a little more to give to get his or her team, organization, or business to a championship level. The remainder of the presentation involves the ideas that drive this book to share the strategies to make a team perform at championship level.

The main role of a coach, leader, CEO, or boss is to make the group believe in themselves. Think back to your favorite teacher or coach. Although as you thought of that person you may have recalled how much you liked him or her, the real reason why that person came into your thoughts was because the belief he or she built in you. If that favorite teacher of coach had asked you to make a change, you would have done so and you would have believed that what was being asked of you would make you better.

Yet when leaders think of what they need to do to be effective, many terms come to mind other than *building belief*. How does a leader build belief? Surely there are essential facets that are important to create the foundation on which to build belief. Certainly, your favorite teacher/coach was organized and had a vision and a game plan to carry out that vision. You can be equally sure that this leader was knowledgable or even an expert in the subject area or sport and possessed a consistent energy to carry out the mission.

Your favorite coach or teacher built a good foundation by identifying core values and then identifying behaviors that reinforced those core values. The teacher communicated well and consistently. The teacher was enjoyable to listen to, and you appreciated feedback. The way the teacher reinforced and communicated with you matched your personality and motivated you to get better.

Performing those facets of leadership well also builds an employee's belief in the leader. However, most leaders leave it there. To "fill the gap," leaders have to be aggressive in planning the strategies that will constantly work to build belief in their employees. Instead of hoping team members have a high level of belief, leaders must have a plan to increase the level of belief in their employees to get the team to perform at the highest level possible.

As much as data analysis might shape the activities and processes a company goes through, teams need to go through activities that give the members a clear message on how to believe at a higher level. These activities are the ones that make championship teams. In presenting to organizations, I like to give ideas for activities that teams can use to directly increase their level of belief, abolish limitations, and get to a performance level that represents a potential higher than anyone believed was possible.

I encourage leaders to have "leadership themes" that they present to their teams to help shape their mentality. There needs to be a perspective toward individual and team performance that gives a clear message of what is necessary to be a championship team. The amount of time that is spent on developing these themes and schemes to motivate and impact team members may even be greater than the time spent on other factors of production.

UNBELIEVABLE

"Unbelievable" is my favorite word in sports psychology. The word has so much power and significance. An athlete or team may have their best performance and think of it as "unbelievable." Or, in thinking of what can be done in a sport, people will label a level of performance as "unbelievable," limiting the potential that someone else could be capable of achieving or exceeding that same level. Most of the time, even the inflection in someone's voice is telling. When many use this word, it is often dragged out to sound even more unattainable, "unnnbelieeeevable."

For someone to believe, they need to be open to hearing about what the possibilities actually are, rather than dealing with the fact that some possibilities are just "unbelievable." If a group believes a level of performance is unbelievable, they have limited their chance of achieving that level. Steve Jobs was famous for pushing his employees to do what they had labeled as impossible.

In order to make the "unbelievable," "believable," the issue that must immediately be addressed is ego. Individuals driven by ego will often hold fast to old ways or previously held limitations. Their ego must often be maintained even in the face of new information.

One of my first business presentations was to a vice president's team in a major corporation that was a $25 billion Fortune 500 corporation. I was speaking on how to build belief in an organization and its employees. Before the presentation I had an envelope placed in front of each of the participants, and a waste basket in the middle of this circle of business leaders. When I addressed the group, I began by asking them to put their egos aside for forty-five minutes so that they could better understand belief building.

We were in agreement that we should not allow our "ego to be the enemy," a borrowed Ryan Holiday phrase, in dealing with new possibilities. In the envelope, each member of the group found a piece of paper that had the word, "ego," printed in large text on the paper. The group was asked to put their ego aside so they could listen with their heart to the idea of abolishing limitations. As corny as this all may sound, the participants were then to crumble up their papers and throw their ego in the garbage. By dispensing of their egos, they were now open to the possibilities presented in presentation.

The fourth national championship we won at Springfield College was a great win against the University of California Santa Cruz (UCSC). The Springfield team demonstrated their belief in the form of mental fortitude during this national championship match. UCSC has been the number one seed all season and Springfield had lost the first match of the year to them 0–3. Things did not get better in the championship, as Springfield lost the first set of the match.

Being down 0–1, and being the lower-seeded team, Springfield needed all the belief possible at this point. Not only so our players could believe more *but so their players would believe less*. One of the most powerful effects of believing in yourself is that it lowers your opponent's level of belief. Springfield was revived by a heightened belief and went on to win that national championship in four sets.

Perhaps no recent sporting success reinforces this idea of building a culture of belief more than UMBC's surprise victory over Virginia in the 2018 NCAA tournament, the first time a 16 seed had beaten a number 1 seed in NCAA Division I history. In an analysis of this victory by UMBC professor Freeman Hrabowski, the idea of winning the game of belief comes to life.

> Even though they had lost 23 games in a row to Vermont, we could win the 24th and the America East Conference championship. An attitude that said that, despite the odds, they could beat Virginia, an outstanding team from one of the oldest, wealthiest, and most-respected public institutions in the country.

The professor goes on to share the how of the upset: "What makes our story so appealing is that the players not only have a strong sense of self, they have hope. It is not idle hope. . . . Rigorous preparation can lead people to reach goals they didn't think were possible."

What is most striking about the win is not the basketball improbability, but the fact that this win was part of a mission of the college to inspire belief beyond the basketball courts.

> We've defied the odds before. Three decades ago, nobody believed you could close the achievement gap between white and underrepresented minority students, who were disproportionately likely to be lower-income and to be less academically prepared, without adjusting academic standards. . . . We believed you could set high expectations and, with appropriate support, not only help minority students succeed but also excel in some of the toughest fields.

Today, graduating students of all races and income levels, UMBC sees its students go on to earn PhDs and join the faculties of some of the most prestigious institutions in the country, from Harvard to Duke.

Any team, organization, or group working to achieve a goal and have great task cohesion together needs to "fill the gap" that exists between what their best performance actually is and what they currently think their best performance is. This is not something that happens by accident, but will only come into existence through the conscious efforts of the leaders to build belief.

The stories in this book were shared to inspire you to create your own stories and strategies to build belief in your organization, whether those organizations exist in a classroom, on a field or court, or in the boardroom. The stories that have driven this book have all arisen from my need to create belief in my team. Now, it is time for you to make your own stories to create belief in your team.

Five Takeaways from *Raise Your Hand: Applications to Business*

1. There is an achievement gap between what people believe is their maximum performance and what that level of performance actually is.
2. Most people have limited their own performance by their belief that only certain levels of performance are possible.
3. Society uses the word "unbelievable" in ways that make it seem that extraordinary performance is a level that is beyond human potential.
4. In order to open yourself to the belief that new levels of performance are possible, you first have to give up your ego that may hold fast to even the possibility that new levels of performance are attainable.
5. Successful organizations are successful because they have a higher level of belief that they will succeed than their competitors.

The Big Idea from *Raise Your Hand: Applications to Business*

Leaders need to focus on and develop the methods that they will use to build belief in their employees as much as they concentrate on the data analysis and product development. The belief that there are no limits to performance goals cannot be achieved without an explicit design by the leader.

A Dozen Big Ideas to Move Your Organization beyond Inspiration

Idea One: Brain research has discovered that the most effective way to communicate messages that will impart deep and lasting belief in an organization is through the power of stories. The secrets of winning the game of belief will be shared through the power of the stories that begin each chapter.

Idea Two: Organizations that win all the time foster in their members an unshakable belief that they will triumph in the end. *They win the game of belief.* This belief is tested on a daily basis, and the role of any leader is to arm his members with the belief that they can overcome any obstacle or challenge that they face in their pursuit of excellence.

Idea Three: Teams that win all the time possess a stronger belief that they will win than the teams that they face. In the end, it is this belief that leads to success.

Idea Four: Truly successful leaders find opportunity in the obstacles that they face. In fact, the key to maintaining belief is the ability to view a setback as an opportunity for growth and to embrace the virtues that emerge as a result of the setback.

Idea Five: Winning leaders need to select individuals for their organizations on more than natural talent. Successful organizations need to measure the personality traits of the individual and gauge belief, effort, and will in the individual if they want to build championship organizations.

Idea Six: What all great leaders define for their organizations are a set of clearly articulated core values that drive every decision and action of the organization. These core values are often born of previous failures and setbacks by the leader. Struggles and life lessons make the core values more than words on paper.

Idea Seven: Gritty cultures share core values that nurture grit. These cultures are defined by a shared belief and effort on the part of the individuals that make up the culture, a product-over-process orientation, and an identity with the culture, making team goals more important than individual goals.

Idea Eight: Cultures of belief are built on the work ethic of the coach, which results in a mutual work ethic by players. These cultures are transformative for their members, who are actualized as players and as people as a result of being part of the culture.

Idea Nine: The focus for winning teams is always on process, seeking to perfect that process rather than the short-term results of that process.

Idea Ten: When organizations are truly successful in creating a culture of belief, participants in that culture enjoy a relationship with the organization that creates their purpose and identity in life and a motivation that puts team goals in front of personal goals.

Idea Eleven: For organizations to be truly successful, leaders must not only create and communicate core values, but they must also maintain those values when they are challenged. Those values must become the deciding factors in every decision that the organization makes and in every direction that the organization undertakes.

Idea Twelve: Leaders need to focus on and develop the methods that they will use to build belief in their employees as much as they concentrate on the data analysis and product development. The belief that there are no limits to performance goals cannot be achieved without an explicit design by the leader.

Appendix A

The NFL Draft: How Did You Do?

The other candidates that you chose in our NFL draft exercise became pretty good quarterbacks in their own right. You can check below to see which quarterback you would have selected with your first pick as a general manager in the draft exercise. The exercise should reveal to you that the unmeasured characteristics of passion for the goal driven by belief and effort may be even more important than the statistics below.

Table A.1.   NFL Draft Selections Revealed

Name	40 Yard Dash	20 Yard Shuffle	3 Cone Drill	Vertical Leap
Candidate 1 Cam Newton	4.56	4.18	6.92	35
Candidate 2 Russell Wilson	4.53	4.09	6.97	34
Candidate 3 Colin Kaepernick	4.53	4.18	6.85	32.5
Candidate 4 Matt Ryan	4.89	4.51	7.1	24.5
Candidate 5 Tony Romo	5.01	4.2	7.11	30
Candidate 6 Tom Brady	5.28	4.38	7.2	24.5
Candidate 7 Andrew Luck	4.59	4.28	6.8	36

Appendix B

April Bus Rides: The Players in Their Own Words

In our *me*-obsessed world, maybe the idea of culture and April volleyball is all too much for you to swallow at this time. Could be that these stories are made up or exaggerated to boost the sales of the book. To truly authenticate the values that define this program at Springfield, there was no other way but to share the actual words of the players themselves.

Meeting Charlie in the locker room on the eve of one of his championships, I noticed the walls of the locker room covered with emails from alumni about their experiences on the April bus ride. As I walked around and started to read what alumni had written about their experience, I realized that I had all the evidence needed to bring the lessons of *Winning the Game of Belief* to life.

As Charlie took down some of the emails and handed them to me, I realized that these testimonies to the experience of being a part of Springfield volleyball were all the proof that I needed on the impact of this culture on the players' lives. I chose to submit them exactly as they were written.

Below are six of the letters that surrounded that locker room. They speak more powerfully to the power of culture and why some coaches win all the time than I or this book ever could. To conclude the appendix, there are some final thoughts on getting on the April Bus by Coach Sullivan that capture the philosophy that this book attempts to share.

Tyler Wingate   Apr 24 (1 day ago)

to me

Hi Coach,

Hope you and the team are doing well.

It's an exciting time of year and I know you and the guys are preparing to play championship level volleyball this weekend. It has been great to come into a few practices this year along with being at some matches and see the level of commitment to getting better every day.

I think back to the year 2008 and I was in my sophomore year at SC. That year we had been selected to host the Molten National Championship along with three other teams. I was able to experience the championship feel the year before when we traveled to Juniata College. In 2008 we were hosting and slated to play in the semifinals against that same Juniata team that happened to be the defending national champions. We had the late match that night and I think we were all in a state of shock after watching Vassar upset UC Santa Cruz who had an excellent team that year in the first semifinal. I think it energized us to see that performance from Vassar and to go out in front our the home crowd and play at a high level. We had a great performance that night and won a tightly contested match. I'm sure coach has mentioned the story of Javier Rosario to you before. This was Javier's senior year and this was the weekend that coach references at times because of the sticking to the process, to taking advantage of an opportunity, to just overall BELIEF! It was amazing to be a part of that experience and we carried the momentum from Friday night into a National Championship win on Saturday night. I remember telling Javi after the match how well I thought he played and that I wasn't sure if we would have won if it wasn't for his performance. As humble as he always is he just smiled and said it wasn't just him the team played great tonight and he was so happy to cap off the season with a team performance like that.

Best of luck this weekend fellas. Enjoy the whole experience and all the preparation that goes into it. I look forward to watching you play championship level volleyball this weekend!

Tyler

Figure B.1.   Letter One

James Seitelman   Apr 19 (6 days ago)

to me

Fellas,

These letters never get old. Congratulations on a fantastic regular season, now its April the best time of the year. I am sure the excitement on campus is over the top. Enjoy each moment from the banquet to warm ups to the final point. Each year is its own journey and you never know if your going to get back to this point so you need to take a breath and let it soak in. You have the support of your teammates, family, alumni and the whole SC student body, regardless of the outcome. I was on the 2001 team that won our first championship at SC it was a great experience wining at home. We had our backs against the wall multiple times that April. In the semi finals we were down 10-4 to Vassar and made the improbable comeback to win and then win the championship the following night in 4 sets. The point of that is to remind you that once you put on that SC jersey you can do anything. Have confidence and trust in the process. Seniors... Once you win you have the right to mess up Coach Sullivan's hair I started that tradition and hope that it continues to this day!

Figure B.2.   Letter Two

It is without a doubt the best time of the year in The Mecca. We all know it.

As you read all of the e-mails pouring in from ghosts of SCVB's past, we all send similar messages that are so important at this stage in the season.

BELIEF. TRUST. TEAM. and most importantly, **PROCESS.**

This group has been battle tested, not only this year but in recent years as well. I know you guys are hungry to get going here in a couple days and maybe a little bit nervous. This is where the PROCESS takes over. Remember back to those practices where you were grinding out the smallest change in your game, the specific play you made that change, and the all of the hard work to become a better player. That is where you guys learned the most important lessons and now is the time to reflect back on that and use that experience this weekend.

To be successful this weekend it takes **EVERY PERSON** on the roster. Know your role and if you continue to give yourself to your teammates and coaches, this weekend can be something special. TRUST your teammates, TRUST Coach Sullivan, **BELIEVE** in in everything you've worked so hard for.

Enjoy every moment; especially you seniors, there just isn't anything like it!

WE SLAY!

Ryan Lilley, '14

Figure B.3.   Letter Three

Becker, Michael   10:58 AM (36 minutes ago)
to me

Fellas,

It's that time of year again! The April bus is rolling and no one truly understands the benefits that SC gets when April rolls around. To every person not repping SCVB, April is just another month – but to us, it's something incredibly special. It's a time where the team truly buys in to the process and their rolls. I graduated 4 years ago till now and every time April rolls around I still get the chills.

I can't describe how much each of you have a roll to fill and how each roll plays an important part in the journey. Whether you are a starter, come in for just a few points, or are on the sidelines, each person plays a vital roll come April. My personal experience, my senior year, was as much of a roller coaster ride as you could imagine. After starting every match my senior year and setting the team to the highest hitting % in DIII, I was told that I would not be a starter for the finals but could go in to serve if I was comfortable enough. To this day, that was one of the hardest things I've ever been told and I'll remember that moment for the rest of my life. However, as the new shirts say, "In Charlie We Trust." The dude knows what it takes to play at a high level and knows how to get the most out of you no matter what that may be.

Trust in the process and buy in! April is a special moment for you all and SCVB alums around the world. Rock the Mecca!

   **Mike Becker**

Figure B.4.   Letter Four

Brethren,

On April 2, 2012 I stumbled my scrawny, freshman body up the ramp of Blake, thinking practice had been moved to Dana because the faint sound of Kool & The Gang's "Celebration" which grew louder and louder as I neared the top of the ramp. I turn the corner and to my viewing pleasure is the one and only, Coach Sullivan, standing on a hitting box, rocking out with his air guitar with some intermittent, "Happy April Volleyball" shouts as I made my way into the gym (if only you were still rockin the mullet, Coach). At this moment, I knew how special 'April Volleyball' was to the program and how it had contributed to the success the SCVB family has had during this month.

April is a time of celebration. We celebrate the successes of the season, the excitement of potential post-season play, but one thing the program is great at during this time is celebrating the setbacks we have overcome, the areas we still need to improve in, and celebrating the ability to acknowledge that we all still have room to grow. I remember sitting in Schaaf at the end of April, watching film from pre-season and comparing it to how much better our blocking, offense and defense had gotten while also listening to Coach point out areas that still need work. Now is the time to recognize how far you have come, but realize and commit to where you can go from here. You are in control -- you can make it happen.

You will likely remember a few matches and, if you're lucky, maybe even a few specific plays that are special and mean a lot when you look back on your time with SCVB. What I can guarantee is that you will remember the family you spent your Aprils with for these four years of your life. There are very few times, if any, after you leave Springfield that you will be part of a group of people who all share the same interests as you and have the same goals. Your brothers, and all the ones who came before you, have challenged each other to develop and become a better athlete, but silently and without ever really noticing, you are all shaping each other into the men you are becoming. Be the best man you can be for the others around you.

I would not be where I am today if not for the community at Springfield, but more importantly, the family I have thanks to SCVB. Know that you will forever have a support system with SCVB, past, present and future once you leave Springfield. Seniors, I look forward to watching in the stands with you next year, but this is your time – go get it. Young bloods, I look forward to watching you grow as volleyball players and men during your time at SC. I plan to watch at some point every season until I'm old and wheelchair bound (and let's face it, that could be sooner than we think haha).

You all know what needs to be done, and no program in the country trains or prepares like Springfield. Be focused, play hard for your family on the court and in the stands, and enjoy playing post-season April volleyball in The Mecca. Damn, it doesn't get any better than that.

Love you all,

Keaton (not king) Pieper ;)

Figure B.5. Letter Five

Ufff Coach, I woke up today with so much positivity and realized it was April Volleyball. I was ultimately overfilled with joy and excitement the second it turned to April 1.

Earlier today, I had a gym session with bunch of guys from the team. As our workout continued, my teammates were wondering why I was so motivated and energized. I kept telling them " Men, it's April" ,the best time of the year. After I explained them what "April" meant to me, they got very encouraged and were all aboard to ride the bus with me. We created a great environment and dominated our gym session.

I was excited to see all of my teammates buying in and working harder. It was a great feeling to be able to influence others by such little things, something as simple as telling them about April Volleyball. I learned that it is beneficial to take the little things in volleyball as well as life and make them really stand out. However, that is in the control of each and every person and what choices they choose to make in order to keep the positive energy, motivation, and determination ongoing.

As you are a very important person in my life, I wanted to tell you a story that has happened to me during my season in Germany...My teammates are all extremely talented professional volleyball players with a lot of experience coming from their prior national teams. I knew I was going to be challenged with great competition the minute I signed the contract to play. I was ecstatic about the new journey in my life and to be able to play against great players. I knew it would take a lot of work but I was willing to put everything I had, to any adversity that came along the way.

Every practice I was so motivated to be great and give my maximum effort. I was pushing the other players in my position to play even harder because I wanted to challenge them. The second team in practice was beating the starting line up every time; we wanted to push the starting side to be even better. Last month we had an extremely tough schedule, and I knew my chances to start were low because we were winning. However, one game the coach asked me to come in to serve for the middle during crunch time in a 5 setter. I did not hesitate and was so hyped to come in the game. I knew I needed to trust myself. I could not overthink and think that I was going to miss the serve. I was in my zone and feeling more confident than ever. The score was 23-23 and I got two aces to win the game. Man, it felt so good to show my team and coaches that they can trust me and I was ready to embrace the moment.

Last week, we played the top team in the league and we needed to win in order to keep our standing in the top 3. This was important for us so that we could move up to the first league for the next year. Before the game, the coach called me up during warmups and said to me " You know you are starting today right!? I told him.. " I'm ready". I was so excited to finally have my chance. We beat the top team 3-0 to secure a spot in the first league next year. Coach, all of the hard work I put in has finally paid off.

The reason I wanted to share this story with you is that no matter what your coach wants you to do, you have to be ready and give all you got. It's about trusting the process, and learning not only to be a better player but to a be a better person. It's about knowing that we all are prepared to succeed with the right mindset; keeping the positive energy going, being motivated, and influencing others to have the right attitude. And that Coach is what April Volleyball is all about. It's about making changes, accepting the change, building better relationships, and no matter what, giving your best at any second. Because, you may not know, but you can influence others by such little things.

Thank you Coach, you have helped me to succeed by your philosophy of April Volleyball. I have been able to become a better athlete because of your insights. And I am so thankful for that because I can apply your guidance to make me a better person and look at life in a different way.

HAPPY APRIL VOLLEYBALL

Figure B.6. Letter Six

How can you make it onto the court at TD Garden and be "honored" for a championship level process?

1) **Body language** is the first language for SCVB. It doesn't matter where you are from.
2) Everyone needs to put in 100% of their **effort** at all times. The more you put into practices and continue to get better, the more the team will benefit from it.
3) Take every moment of **adversity** as an opportunity to grow and improve.
4) Holding back on a personal goal that you have is the most selfish thing you can do in this program. Whatever you guys do, do it with the intention of helping someone else.
5) Everyone must be hungry to play **April** volleyball. The energy needs to come from everyone, no matter if you are on or off the court.
6) Don't let mistakes take control of your mind and body. Remember, "A mistake is not a mistake until you fail to correct it."
7) Buy into the process with total **trust**. Understand your role in this program, and be ready for that to change at any moment.

Figure B.7.   Charles Sullivan: Making it to the Final Game in April. Author created.

Appendix C

Springfield Core Values
Springfield College Volleyball 2017

VISION
THIS SEASON IS YOUR OPPURTUNITY
"To play 'CHAMPIONSHIP LEVEL' volleyball"
Springfield College Men's Volleyball

CORE VALUES

1) Work hard to win every rally
2) Have your actions enhance our team cohesion
3) Build relationships by communicating and listening
4) Have a learning mindset and be process oriented
5) Compete every day, making yourself and others better
6) Stay connected to the fundamentals you need to improve

Show up every day fully engaged. Be in the moment. How persistent your work toward improving is will determine your success.

THE HOW = ACTION

- FAST—Dominating
- EFFICIENT—Statistically great
- GREAT COMMUNICATION—Body language/ mouth and eyes
- FUNDAMENTALLY SOUND—Great skills
- BELIEF—100% available, take it all (2nd time!)

CULTURE/ BEHAVIORS

1. Process-over-product orientations
2. Cohesion
3. Represent
4. Effort
5. Tough
6. Expectations
7. Statistics

PROCESS OVER PRODUCT

- The processes are the roots of our program. The results are the fruits.
- We need to water the roots, enjoy the fruits, and then quickly refocus on taking care of the roots some more.
- We control the process—effort, connection to our objectives, attitude, self-talk, process goals (70% PP ex.), communication
- We have no control over product—officials, competition, 1 inch
- Competing in practice, cauldron, positional ranks, and TEAM RESULTS are products. Do not be distracted by these, and get back into the process. Ex: Javier Rosario
- Be humble about our success and always thankful for our opportunity.

COHESION

- TEAM COHESION—Social cohesion, relationships, and task cohesion are achieved together. Work better together. Your needs are secondary to the program.
- The first time we won 3 National Championships in a row every player was asked the same question after each season. "Why were we so successful?" All but one player, 99%, answered the same. "Team cohesion." At that point we realized how important working on our team cohesion was, and it is not a behavior that Springfield College Volleyball regards lightly.

REPRESENT

- Springfield College Volleyball is a 1st class organization and behavior always represents this. "He is a good kid." "He is a SC kid."
- Take responsibility. Be responsible for your actions and behaviors.

- Be responsible for your failures and accept that weakness leads to improvement.
- Represent yourself, your family, and the program exceptionally.
- Have sportsmanship.
- Use humanics—a strong mentality.

EFFORT

- Effort is the key to everything you do.
- Emphasize effort. To overemphasize talent is to underemphasize everything else, therefore talent is secondary. "Genius" is insulting.
- Talent x Effort = Skill
- Skill x Effort = Achievement
- How much effort can you apply to that equation?
- Stay in love with giving effort—PASSION
- Discipline and accountability are doing the right thing at the right time and that is not a bad thing! Enjoy the fruits and then go back to applying effort!

TOUGHNESS

- Springfield College Volleyball Definition = Limitless, no ceiling—fight through obstacles to get there, no matter how big. There is no giving up.
- Truly mental—Every time a match is won, at one point in that match the minds of the losing team gave up and became weaker.
- Toughness is more important than talent any day, but to mix talent with toughness is the combination that is our goal. UNBELIEVABLE!
- Aggressive play creates luck and fosters BELIEF. We believe more and so does our opponent.
- When expectations are high, tough players only see two choices:
  1) To meet them
  2) To exceed them
- A setback is a set up for a comeback!

EXPECTATIONS

- Culture defines behaviors.
- Understand our culture and how we behave. Ex: Be on time, sit in the front row, go to class, dive for balls, show effort in the weight room, follow the rules of the training room, etc.

- Follow all policies of the campus and dorms.
- Play other sports.
- Achieve your best grades.
- Prioritize your schedule—avoid procrastinating assignments and stress. Sleep and eat well to get the most out of your performance.

STATISTICS

1) Indicator—Statistics indicate what we need to take responsibility for that is a weakness and they indicate how much we need to improve.
2) Goals—These process goals are great to focus on (70% PP ex.)
3) COMPETE!—We compare player statistics every day (Product) to see who is more efficient (Team Vision). Competition is defined as, "Striving together." It makes everyone better. The product is always going to be there automatically. Using statistics in our program helps us practice not focusing on the numbers, but getting back into the PROCESS. Competing helps every player on the team improve.

SPRINGFIELD COLLEGE VOLLEYBALL FAMOUS QUOTES

- "A mistake is not a mistake until we fail to correct it."
- "Failure is fertilizer for our success."
- "There is no purer evaluation than a loss."
- "We are not afraid of losing, winning is what scares us."
- "Process vs. Product Orientation."
- "Building a wall is about how perfectly we can lay one brick at a time."
- "Good enough is neither good nor enough!"
- "There are only two options regarding commitment. You are either in or you are out. There is no such thing as life in-between."
- "Discipline is doing what you are supposed to do at the right time and that is not a bad thing. Discipline is not a negative word."

Bibliography

Allen, J. *No You Can't, Yes I Can*. Charleston, SC: Self-published: Printed by CreateSpace, 2015.

Andreae, G. *Giraffes Can't Dance*. New York: Scholastic Books, 2012.

Baltzell, A. *Living in the Sweet Spot: Preparing for Performance in Sport and Life*. Morgantown, WV: Fitness Information Technology, 2011.

Bandura, A. (1977). "Self-Efficacy: Toward a Unifying Theory of Behavioral Change." *Psychological Review* 84, no. 2 (1977): 191–215.

Beaty, A. *Iggy Peck, Architect*. New York: Abrams Books for Young Readers, 2007.

———. *Rosie Revere, Engineer.* New York: Abrams Books for Young Readers, 2013.

Catalanotto, P. *Emily's Art*. New York: Atheneum Books for Young Readers, 2006.

Cooperrider, D. L., F. Barrett, and S. Srivastva. "Social Construction and Appreciative Inquiry: A Journey in Organizational Theory." In *Management and Organization: Relational Alternatives to Individualism*, edited by Dian Marie Hosking, H. Peter Dachler, and Kenneth J. Gergen,157–200. Belfast, Northern Ireland: Avebury Press, 1995.

Cooperrider, D. L., and Whitney, D. *Appreciative Inquiry: A Positive Revolution in Change.* San Francisco: Berrett-Koehler Publishers, 2005.

Csikszentmihalyi, M. *Flow: The Psychology of Optimal Experience*. New York: HarperCollins, 1990.

Danielson, C. "One to Grow On: Teaching Like a Four-Star Chef." *Educational Leadership* 70, no. 4 (2014): 90–91.

Dorrance, A., and G. Averbuch. *The Vision of a Champion: Advice and Inspiration from the World's Most Successful Women's Soccer Coach.* Chelsea, MI: Sleeping Bear Press, 2002.

Duckworth, A. L. "Angela Duckworth: The Key to Success: Grit?" Video file. Ted Talks, May 9, 2013. Retrieved from http://www.ted.com/talks/angela_lee_duckworth _the_key_to_success_grit.html.

———. "Angela Duckworth: True Grit: Can Perseverance Be Taught?" Video file. YouTube, October 18, 2009. Retrieved from http://www.youtube.com/watch ?v=qaeFnxSfSC4.

———. "Can Perseverance Be Taught?" *Big Questions Online*, August 5, 2013. Retrieved from https://www.bigquestionsonline.com/content/can-perseverance-be -taught.

———. *Grit: Passion and Perseverance.* New York: Scribner, 2016.

———. "(Over and) Beyond High-Stakes Testing." *American Psychologist* 64, no. 4 (2009): 279–80.

Duckworth, A. L., H. Grant, B. Loew, G. Oettingen, and P. M. Gollwitzer. "Self-Regulation Strategies Improve Self-Discipline in Adolescents: Benefits of Mental Contrasting and Implementation Intentions." *Educational Psychology* 31, no. 1 (2011): 17–26.

Duckworth, A. L., C. Peterson, M. D. Matthews, and D. R. Kelly. "Grit: Perseverance and Passion for Long-Term Goals." *Journal of Personality and Social Psychology* 92, no. 6 (2007): 1087–1101.

Duckworth, A. L., and P. D. Quinn. "Development and Validation of the Short Grit Scale. *Journal of Personality Assessment* 91, no. 2 (2009): 166–74.

Duckworth, A. L., and M. E. P. Seligman. "Self-Discipline Outdoes IQ in Predicting Academic Performance of Adolescents." *American Psychological Society* 16, no. 12 (2005): 939–44.

Dweck, C. S. *Mindset: How You Can Fulfill Your Potential.* London: Hachette UK, 2012.

———. *Mindset: The New Psychology of Success.* New York: Ballantine, 2012.

———. "The Perils and Promises of Praise." *Kaleidoscope, Contemporary and Educational Leadership* 65, no. 2 (2007): 34–39.

———. *Self-Theories: Their Role in Motivation, Personality, and Development.* New York: Psychology Press, 2000.

Dweck, C. S., and D. C. Molden. "Self-Theories: Their Impact on Competence Motivation and Acquisition." In *Handbook of Competence and Motivation*, edited by A. J. Elliot and C. S. Dweck, 135–54. New York: Guildford, 2005.

Farr, R. Once Upon a Time, When There Were No Tests, Children Built Houses That Stood Tall. and Straight . . ." Internet Archive, May 1993. Retrieved August 28, 2015, from https://archive.org/stream/ERIC_ED364850/ERIC_ED364850_djvu.txt.

Farr, R., and B. Tone. "The King and His Carpenters." 1998. Retrieved from http:// users.metu.edu.tr/eryilmaz/Courses/SCE410/King_Carpenter.htm.

Frederickson, B. L. *Love 2.0: How Our Supreme Emotion Affects Everything We Feel, Think, Do and Become.* New York: Hudson Street Press, 2009.

———. *Positivity.* New York: Crown.

Fredrickson, B. L., and M. F. Losada. "Positive Affect and the Complex Dynamics of Human Flourishing." *American Psychologist* 60, no. 7 (2005): 678.

Hafer, T., ed. *Life Wisdom from Coach Wooden: Inspiring Thoughts from the UCLA Coaching Legend.* Ventura, CA: Hallmark Books, 2008.

Holiday, R. *The Obstacle Is the Way: The Ancient Art of Turning Adversity into Advantage.* London: Profile Books, 2014.

Huang, C. A., and J. Lynch. *Thinking Body, Dancing Mind: Taosports for Extraordinary Performance in Athletics, Business and Life.* New York: Bantam Books, 1992.

Jordan, D. and R. M. Jordan. *Salt in His Shoes: Michael Jordan in Pursuit of a Dream.* New York: Simon & Schuster Books for Young Readers, 2003.

Jordan, M. *Driven from Within.* New York: Atria Books, 2005.

Lopez, S. J. *Hope, Academic Success, and the Gallup Student Poll.* Gallup, Inc., 2009. Retrieved from: www.gallupstudentpoll.com/File/122192.

———. "Making Hope Happen in the Classroom." *Phi Delta Kappan* 93, no. 8 (2012): 72–73.

———. *Making Hope Happen: Create the Future You Want for Yourself and Others.* New York: Simon & Schuster, 2013.

———. "Making Ripples of Hope." *Educational Horizons* 89, no. 4 (2011): 9–13.

Lopez, S. J., C. R. Snyder, J. L. Magyar-Moe, L. Edwards, J. T. Pedrotti, K. Janowski, J. L. Turner, J. L . . . and C. Pressgrove. (2004). "Strategies for Accentuating Hope." In *Positive Psychology in Practice,* edited by P. A. Linley and S. Joseph, 388–404. Hoboken, NJ: John Wiley & Sons.

Lovell, P. *Stand Tall, Molly Lou Melon.* New York: G.P. Putnam's Sons, 2001.

Ludwig, T. *Too Perfect.* Berkeley, CA: Tricycle Press, 2009.

Lyubomirsky, S. *The How of Happiness: A Scientific Approach to Getting the Life You Want.* New York: Penguin, 2008.

———. "Why Are Some People Happier Than Others? The Role of Cognitive and Motivational Processes in Well-Being." *Social Indicators Research* 56, no. 3 (2001): 239–49.

Lyubomirsky, S., and H. S. Lepper. "A Measure of Subjective Happiness: Preliminary Reliability and Construct Validation." *Social Indicators Research* 46 (1997): 137–15.

Lyubomirsky, S., and L. Ross. "Hedonic Consequences of Social Comparison: A Contrast of Happy and Unhappy People." *Journal of Personality and Social Research* 73 (1997): 1141–57.

McDermott, D., and S. Hastings. "Children: Raising Future Hopes." In *Handbook of Hope*, edited by C. R. Snyder, 185–99. San Diego: Academic Press, 2000.

McDermott, D., and C. R. Snyder. *Making Hope Happen: A Workbook for Turning Possibilities into Realities.* Oakland, CA: New Harbinger Publications, 1999.

McMullen, K. *Noel the First.* New York: Michael di Capua Books, 1996.

Merriam, E. *The Wise Woman and Her Secret.* New York: Simon & Schuster Children's Publishing, 1991.

Park, N., C. Peterson, and M. E. Seligman. "Strengths of Character and Well-Being." *Journal of Social and Clinical Psychology* 23, no. 5 (2004): 603–19.

Nater, S., and R. Gallimore. *You Haven't Taught until They Have Learned: John Wooden's Teaching Principles and Practices.* Morgantown, WV: Fitness Information Technology, 2006.

Oaklander, M. "The Science of Bouncing Back." *Time*, May 21, 2015.

Parr, T. *It's OK to Make Mistakes.* New York: Little, Brown Books for Young Readers, 2014.

Pearpoint, J., J. O'Brien, and M. Forest. *PATH: A Workbook for Planning Positive Possible Futures: Planning Alternative Tomorrows with Hope for Schools, Organizations, Business, Families.* Toronto: Inclusion Press, 1993.

Peterson, C., and M. E. Seligman. *Character Strengths and Virtues: A Handbook and Classification.* Oxford: Oxford University Press, 2004.

Pett, M., and G. Rubenstein. *The Girl Who Never Made Mistakes.* Naperville, IL: Sourcebooks Jaberwocky.

Pierce, C. *Moving the Chains: Tom Brady and the Pursuit of Everything.* New York: Farrar, Straus and Giroux, 2006.

Pink, D. H. *Drive: The Surprising Truth about What Motivates Us.* New York: Penguin, 2011.

Quinn, R. E. *Deep Change: Discovering the Leader Within.* Hoboken, NJ: John Wiley & Sons, 2010.

———. *The Positive Organization: Breaking Free from Conventional Cultures, Constraints, and Beliefs.* Oakland, CA: Berrett Koehler, 2015.

Rath, T. *Are You Fully Energized? The 3 Keys to Energizing Your Work and Life.* San Francisco: Silicon Guild, 2015.

———. *Eat, Move, Sleep: How Small Changes Lead to Big Changes.* San Francisco: Missionday, 2013.

———. *How Full Is Your Bucket? For Kids.* New York: Gallup Press, 2009.

———. *Strengthsfinder 2.0.* New York: Gallup Press, 2007.

Ravin, I. *The Hoops Whisperer: On the Court and Inside the Heads of Basketball's Best Players.* New York: Gotham Books, 2014.

Reynolds, P. *Going Places.* New York: Atheneum Books for Young Readers, 2014.

Ritchhart, R., M. Church, and K. Morrison. *Making Thinking Visible: How to Promote Engagement, Understanding, and Independence for All Learners.* San Francisco: Jossey-Bass, 2011.

Seligman, M. E. *Flourish: A Visionary New Understanding of Happiness and Well-Being.* New York: Simon & Schuster, 2012.

Shen, L., C. Hsee, J. Zhang, and X. Dai. "Belittling Can Be Flattering." *NA-Advances in Consumer Research* 38 (2011).

Solarz, P. *Learn Like a Pirate: Empower Your Students to Collaborate, Lead and Succeed.* San Diego: Dave Burgess Consulting, 2015.

Snyder, C. R. "Hope Theory: Rainbows in the Mind." *Psychological Inquiry* 13, no. 4 (2002): 249–75.

Snyder, C. R., C. Harris, J. R. Anderson, S. A. Holleran, L. M. Irving, L. M.., S. T. Sigmund, and P. Harney. "The Will and the Ways: Development and Validation of the Individual-Differences Measure of Hope." *Journal of Personality and Social Psychology* 60 (1991): 570–85.

Svitak, A. "Adora Svitak: What Adults Can Learn from Kids." Video File. YouTube, April 2, 2010. Retrieved from https://www.youtube.com/watch?v=V-bjOJzB7LY.

Tough, P. *How Children Succeed: Grit, Curiosity and the Hidden Power of Character.* New York: Houghton Mifflin, 2012.

———. "Who Gets to Graduate?" *New York Times*, May 15, 2014.

Yamaguchi, K. *Dream Big, Little Pig!* Naperville, IL: Sourcebooks Jaberwocky, 2011.

Yeager, D. S., and C. S. Dweck. "Mindsets That Promote Resilience: When Students Believe That Personal Characteristics Can Be Developed." *Educational Psychologist* 47, no. 4 (2012): 302–14.

Yeager, J. M., S. W. Fisher, and D. N. Shearon. *Smart Strengths: A Parent-Teacher-Coach Guide to Building Character, Resilience, and Relationships in Youth.* New York: Cogent Publishing, 2014.

About the Authors

Kevin Sheehan, author of *Growing a Growth Mindset: Unlocking Character Strengths Through Children's Literature*, is a tenured associate professor at Molloy College, where he has served on the faculty for over a decade. In another arena of his life, Kevin is an internationally recognized lacrosse coach and has had a distinguished career in this arena. His numerous accomplishments include coaching Adelphi University to three Division II National Championships, the Australian National Lacrosse Team to two Bronze Medals in the World Games, and Massapequa High School to its first New York State Championship on the scholastic level. For his recognition in the coaching arena, Kevin was inducted into the Long Island Metropolitan Branch of the US Lacrosse Hall of Fame in 2006 and the Oceanside Circle of Pride Hall of Fame in 2009.

Charlie Sullivan will enter his twenty-first season as head coach of the men's volleyball team during the 2018–2019 academic year and will once again be an assistant professor of physical education at his alma mater. In twenty previous years at the helm, Springfield has established a pedigree of championship success and has an overall record of 396–181 for a .686 winning percentage. Sullivan's coaching accomplishments include winning an unprecedented eleven national championships at Springfield, winning a Bronze medal in the 2016 Olympics, and leadership and coaching experiences on every level of volleyball. Recently, Sullivan was chosen to receive USA Volleyball's All-Time Great Coach award. One of the most recognized names in men's volleyball, Sullivan became the twenty-seventh recipient of this prestigious award, which goes to an active coach or one that has been retired for less than five years.